How Well Does Your IEP Measure Up?

Quality Indicators
for
Effective Service Delivery

Other quality books published by Starfish Specialty Press:

How To Be A Para Pro: A Comprehensive Training Manual For Paraprofessionals
Diane Twachtman-Cullen
2000

Trevor Trevor
Diane Twachtman-Cullen
1998

For more information regarding these books, please visit our web site at www.starfishpress.com

How Well Does Your IEP Measure Up?

Quality Indicators
for
Effective Service Delivery

Diane Twachtman-Cullen
Jennifer Twachtman-Reilly

Foreword by David L. Holmes, Ed.D.

STARFISH SPECIALTY PRESS

Because it makes a difference to this one

P.O. Box 799
Higganum, CT 06441-0799
www.starfishpress.com

Published in 2002 in the United States of America by Starfish Specialty Press, LLC, PO Box 799, Higganum, CT, 06441-0799

Cover and book design: Patricia Rasch; Cromwell , CT
Cover illustration: Deidre Sassano; New York, NY

Questions regarding this book, including ordering information should be addressed to:

Starfish Specialty Press, LLC
P.O. Box 799
Higganum, CT 06441-0799
Phone: 1-877-STARFISH (1-877-782-7347)
E-mail: info@starfishpress.com
Visit us on the Internet at www.starfishpress.com

Discounts are available for bulk purchases.

ISBN: 0-9666529-2-4

Library of Congress Catalog Card Number: 2001119974

Printed in the United States of America

10 9 8 7 6 5 4 3 2 1

Dedication

For my husband, Jim, in grateful appreciation for his unwavering support and unshakable belief in me. Jim, you light up my life, and bring balance and grand fun into it.

Much love,
Diane

For my husband, Tim, whose love and support has always encouraged me to reach higher and work harder. You are my inspiration.

With all my love,
J

About the Authors

Diane Twachtman-Cullen, Ph.D., CCC-SLP is Executive Director of the Autism & Developmental Disabilities Consultation Center in Higganum, Connecticut. She is a member of the Panel of Professional Advisors of the Autism Society of America, and also serves on the professional advisory boards of the Asperger Syndrome Coalition of the United States, the Asperger Syndrome Education Network, and the Boston Higashi School. A communication disorders specialist and licensed speech-language pathologist, Dr. Twachtman-Cullen is the author of numerous books, articles, and chapters on the subject of autism and related conditions. She provides consultative services and training seminars, internationally, on a variety of topics related to autism spectrum disorders.

Jennifer Twachtman-Reilly, M.S., CCC-SLP is a communication disorders specialist and licensed speech-language pathologist who specializes in working with individuals with autism spectrum disorders and related communication and language impairments. She provides assessment, direct therapy, and consultative services through the Autism & Developmental Disabilities Consultation Center and Sargent Rehabilitation Center. Ms. Twachtman-Reilly has presented workshops and training seminars at the State, regional, and national levels. She serves on the Executive Board of the Rhode Island Speech-Language-Hearing Association, and is author of the chapter, "Improving the Human Condition Through Communication Training in Autism" which appears in the book, *Contemporary Issues in Behavior Therapy: Improving the Human Condition* (1996, J. R. Cautela & W. Ishaq, Eds.).

Authors' Note

This book is written from an educational, not a legal perspective, and is based upon our interpretation of special education law as it relates to IEP development. We fully acknowledge that interpretations of the law may differ from state to state, and from person to person, and that ours relies heavily on our opinion of what is in the best educational interests of the student. This book is in no way intended to advise readers on matters of law, or to serve as a substitute for their obtaining sound legal advice from qualified professionals where it is warranted or desired. Citations to the law are rendered purely for informational purposes, and as a context for our opinions.

Table of Contents

Part One: The Essential Elements of the IEP

Part Two: IEP Goal and Objective Templates

Acknowledgments

First and foremost, we would like to express our deepest gratitude to the students who have inspired this work, and to their families who give eloquent voice to their children's right to appropriate and effective educational services. Rest assured, we hear you! For those educators, clinicians, and enlightened administrators who really "get it," you have our unending admiration and respect. For Nancy Redmond, we really listened when you said, "The two of you should write a book about the IEP." We are grateful to you, not only for the prompt, but also for the wonderful example you set, and for your friendship. Thanks also go to the Volusia County Florida Public Schools and ESE staff for their continued support of our work, and most particularly for giving us the opportunity to address IEP development for its teachers and speech-language clinicians. We are particularly grateful to Heather Cullen for providing the resource materials that made such a difference in this manuscript, and for her all-out effort to place them in our hands at just the right time. We are also grateful to Attorney Walter A. Twachtman, Jr. for his invaluable help regarding all matters legal in this text. To the administration and staff of Sargent Rehabilitation Center's Day School Program in Warwick, Rhode Island: Thank you for the example you set by creating a work environment whose bar is set at excellence. We especially thank Marilyn Serra for her flexibility and understanding regarding our commitment to this project, as well as Patrecia Zebrowski and Michaela Turbitt for sharing their valuable insights regarding occupational therapy. We are most grateful to Susan Twachtman, not only for her editorial assistance, but also for her crucial "regular educator" perspective. Many thanks to our editor Bailey Williams for his unique perspective, and for really "sinking his teeth into this project." We extend a special thank you to Patty Romanowski Bashe for her above and beyond editorial assistance as we went to press. Hats off to Deidre Sassano for her beautifully rendered cover illustration, and to Pat Rasch for lending her talent to the overall design of the front and back covers. We are also grateful to Pat for her invaluable help with the formatting of the book, her quick response time, and her never-ending good humor. Many thanks to Al and Jason Lemire for their cooperation with time lines and all matters related to the printing of this book. We also thank Marylee Thomason of Future Horizons for her assistance with citations and references. Most especially, we are tremendously grateful to the community of exceptional professionals and family members who lent their support to this project by giving of their time, expertise, and eloquence: Dr. David L. Holmes for his exquisite Foreword, Patty Romanowski Bashe, Lee Grossman, Barb Kirby, Dr. Cathy Pratt, and Attorney Peter W.D. Wright, for their insightful comments and inspiring endorsements of this book. We are honored by your presence! And to Erich Twachtman: We, and this book, are enriched by your presence, as well—your attention to detail, dazzling competence, and uncompromising commitment to quality. Last, but by no means least, to our husbands, James T. Cullen, and Timothy M. Reilly: Thank you so very much for your willingness to always go to "alternate plan B" when the book got in the way of plan A. Your esprit de corps has made all the difference.

Foreword

It is with distinct pleasure that I write this Foreword to *How Well Does Your IEP Measure Up?* by Dr. Diane Twachtman-Cullen and her talented daughter Jennifer Twachtman-Reilly. My pleasure stems from two perspectives, the first is the very high regard in which I hold Dr. Twachtman-Cullen as a leading professional in the field of services to those with autism; and, secondly, because I am so impressed with the fact that her daughter, Jennifer Twachtman-Reilly is following her mother's significant lead in serving those with autism by becoming a remarkable professional in her own right.

Throughout the years, as Chairman of the Panel of Professional Advisors for the Autism Society of America I have had the honor to serve with Dr. Twachtman-Cullen and to observe her professional growth and impact on services across this nation for those with autism in public schools, private schools, and on home-bound instruction. Her care and concern for the establishment of effective treatment is noteworthy. Her hands-on approach is unprecedented when compared to others in the field who "theorize" on effective services, but never get their feet wet. Dr. Twachtman-Cullen practices what she preaches, and her practice is of the highest order.

Not too long ago I received a copy of *How To Be A Para Pro: A Comprehensive Training Manual For Paraprofessionals*, authored by Dr. Twachtman-Cullen, and have referenced this book as a leading example of how we in the field of services to those with autism can best utilize the talents and skills of paraprofessionals to augment the services of professionals such as special educators, regular educators, speech pathologists, occupational therapists, physical therapists, and others who enable individuals with autism to grow and become fully included members of society. Now with this new book, *How*

Well Does Your IEP Measure Up?, Dr. Twachtman-Cullen has collaborated with her daughter to take on a very significant issue confronting educators, allied professionals, and families across this nation—the development of appropriate services for children in their care.

A wise person once said, "If you have no direction in life, any road will take you there." This new book will enable those who serve autism to undertake a journey that is sensitive to the needs of the child with autism and his/her family, and to clearly establish the road map necessary to fulfill that journey. Often times I am asked to review IEPs (Individualized Educational Plans) that are aimless in their direction, and that lack the necessary clarity for observable and measurable progress. These IEPs read like an open-ended contract that, for all intents and purposes, allow the practitioner to do whatever he/she feels necessary at the moment, with little or no accountability whatsoever. This book not only sets the foundation for the importance of understanding the unique learning needs of children with autism, but also enables the reader to plan the child's journey of learning, complete with road map and mile markers, to ensure continuous progress along the way. In short, Dr. Diane Twachtman-Cullen and Jennifer Twachtman-Reilly have created a manual that will become indispensable to professionals that serve children with autism and also to their families who will be able to hold "we" in the educational services field more accountable for the progress or lack thereof of the children with autism in our care. This book will be another ray of hope in the lives of children with autism who are amongst our most vulnerable students.

David L. Holmes, Ed.D.
President, The Eden Institute, Inc.
Princeton, NJ

Introduction

It is said that you can't judge a book by its cover. You can, however, tell a great deal about its philosophy and content. In the case of *How Well Does Your IEP Measure Up: Quality Indicators for Effective Service Delivery,* the bar (i.e., standard) against which to "measure" how well a particular individualized education plan (IEP) meets its obligations to the student is not only set at *quality,* but also intimately connected to the *delivery of services* (i.e., outcomes). That pretty much sums up our philosophy and encapsulates what we've tried to accomplish in terms of content. Unfortunately, in our increasingly litigious society, holding up the IEP to *any* standard is enough to conjure up images of due process hearings. That was not our intention in writing this book. While we recognize that in some instances due process may be necessary, we leave the task of directing parents through that arduous procedure to other writers. In fact, we advocate *avoiding* the due process route whenever possible. Toward this end, we offer the reader a sure-fire modus operandi for doing just that—a step-by-step guide to help parents, educators, and clinicians get the right education plan/program in place from the outset, thereby avoiding the need for legal action. Simply stated, this book is about how to write thoughtful, intelligent IEPs that deliver high-quality, need-based educational programming to students with autism spectrum disorders (ASD).

Our focus on the population of students with ASD is threefold. First and foremost, it is our belief that, because of the enigmatic nature of autism, there is a tendency to judge the behavior of these students as willful or volitional, rather than as the outward manifestation of a compromised neurological system. Hence, students with this condition have the most to lose when IEPs fail to take their unique needs and perspectives into account. Secondly, because in ASD things aren't always as they seem, school personnel seem to have an especially difficult task translating goals and objectives into sound educational practices for these students. Finally, our expertise and consultative work in the fields of autism, communication/language disorders, and education provide a useful foundation for addressing issues related to IEP development for students on the autism spectrum.

The underlying premise of this book is that the IEP is the individualized "blueprint" that "drives" appropriate educational programming. As such, like other blueprints, it must contain the exact specifications and conditions necessary to guide the "builders" of educational programs. The organization of the book reflects this premise. To wit, after a brief, but instructive, historical overview of special education law in Chapter 1, the remaining chapters in Part 1 of the book contain the "specs" (i.e., quality indicators) for each of the essential elements of the IEP. Hence, Chapters 2 through 9, respectively, present a carefully ordered and detailed "task analysis" regarding the following crucial building blocks of IEP development: *present levels of performance (PLP); underlying conditions; methodology; criteria for performance/ prompt levels; generalization; goals/objectives; evaluation/ data collection;* and *an IEP potpourri (i.e., least restrictive environment (LRE), accommodations and modifications, related services,* and *supplementary aids and services).* Our goal in Part 1 of the book is to arm the reader with the specific information (i.e., "building specs") needed to generate the types of meaningful goals and objectives that lead to *effective* service delivery.

Part 2 of the book presents several "builder's models," if you will, so that the reader can see how the specs outlined in Part 1 lead to comprehensive, clearly defined IEP goals and objectives. Chapter 10 discusses assessment considerations, particularly as they relate to determining priority educational needs. It also serves as an introduction to Part 2. Chapters 11 through 14, respectively, contain sample PLPs, goals, and objectives related to the following areas of cognitive and social-cognitive functioning: *comprehension; communication, expression, and oral-motor skills; social interaction, play, and leisure skills;* and *cognitive and social cognitive skills (i.e., executive function, critical thinking,* and *theory of mind)*. In addition, we provide the reader with recommended educational programming formats, general teaching tips and strategies, and teaching resources, all of which are designed to help IEP teams translate goals and objectives into sound educational practice. There is also an *Epilogue,* intended to provide a cohesive, concluding statement regarding the crucial link between well-stated IEP goals and objectives and effective service delivery.

Our goal in Part 2 of the book is to put it all together, so that the reader can see, from the many examples given, exactly how the various elements of the IEP can lead to a whole far greater than the sum of its individual parts—*the delivery of an appropriate, individualized education program.* The importance of including practical information related to programming formats, teaching strategies, and resource materials cannot be overstated, particularly since students with ASD require more *specialized* programming than that typically found in "standard special education fare." Support for this position is found in Peeters and Gillberg (1999) who state that the need to adapt education to students with ASD is "perhaps the greatest challenge," (p. 79), given that "traditional" special education programs leave much to be desired for this population. In fact, Peeters and Gillberg (1999) state uncategorically that, "special education which offers the type of teaching used in mental retardation (which consists principally of simplification) does not suffice" (p. 79). Finally, because methodology is the means by which goals and objectives are translated into outcomes for students, it is inextricably intertwined with the standard of appropriateness; that is, methodology either serves as the standard bearer for *appropriate* educational programming, or as the ultimate red flag for *inappropriate* programming!

User-friendly features found within the book are intended to make information both easily accessible and readily useable. These include the use of bullets to streamline information, so that it is clear and concise. Similarly, the liberal use of italics serves as the print version of a highlighter pen for important information.

Finally, *How Well Does Your IEP Measure Up?* is intended for *anyone*—parent or professional—whose ultimate goal is to write high-quality IEPs for students with ASD, at all age and functioning levels, that meet both the letter and *spirit* of the law, and that lead to the delivery of *effective* educational services. That said, it is important to note that while there is only one federal law governing IEP development, there are many interpretations of that law, not only from state to state, but also from one school district to another. Our interpretation relies heavily on the *spirit* of the law, for it is within this dimension that the essence of the individualized education plan may be found. *If there is a bias, it is in the student's favor, for in all issues related to this book we operated from the perspective of what was in the best educational interests of the student with ASD.* Our fondest wish is that the information contained within these pages will enable parents and school personnel to work together, as equal partners, to build educational programs of value for students with autism spectrum disorders.

Diane Twachtman-Cullen
Jennifer Twachtman-Reilly

A journey of a thousand miles begins with the first step.

Chinese Proverb

Part One:

The Essential Elements of the IEP

.

Chapter 1

Past Perspectives, Present Practices

More than a quarter-century ago an event occurred in Washington, D.C. that revolutionized, and forever changed the face of special education services in the United States of America. That event was the enactment of *Public Law 94-142*, the *Education for All Handicapped Children Act (EHA)*. This landmark legislation gave birth to two interrelated concepts. The first was that of a *free appropriate public education (FAPE)*—the legal standard bearer for educational programming for students with disabilities. The second was that of the *individualized education plan (IEP)*. This multifaceted document provided answers to many of special education's most important questions. For example, it specified what was to be taught, and to a large extent the *hows*, the *whens*, and the *wheres* of educational programming for students with special needs (Twachtman-Cullen, 2001).

Having been "born" in the golden era when management by objectives and attention to accountability were the catch phrases of the day, the IEP offered the promise of welcome relief from nebulous, catch-as-catch-can programming. It also offered a systematic approach to educational programming by requiring that educational goals and objectives not only be stated in *outcome-based*, behavioral terms, but also that they be *measurable*. Hence, in addition to the specifications noted in the preceding paragraph, the IEP also emphasized the importance of *data collection* for the purpose of determining how well educational programming was meeting the needs of students with disabilities.

Not all that glittered was golden, however, for neither *autism* nor *pervasive developmental disorder (PDD)* was recognized as a legitimate disability category under the new law. Necessity being the mother of invention, educators and parents soon found ways to finesse services under *P.L. 94-142* by using other disability categories to obtain specialized programming. While some of these labels were relatively innocuous (e.g., *Other Health Impaired)*, for the most part, they left much to be desired in the quest for educational services that were *individualized* to the specific needs of students with autism and related conditions.

The Remarkable Nineties

If *P.L. 94-142* offered a foot in the door marked *FAPE,* the *Individuals with Disabilities Act (IDEA)* pushed that door wide open. The year was 1990. The event was the reauthorization of *P.L. 94-142* under the rubric of *IDEA.* Not only did this law re-affirm the importance of individualized education for students with disabilities, it also granted official status to *autism* as a valid disability category. Hence, for the first time, students with autism and related conditions were able to receive educational services under the label that most accurately reflected their disability and consequently, their needs.

The decade of the nineties marked a fertile period for special education law, given that nine years after the reauthorization of *P.L. 94-142* as *IDEA,* new amendments gave the law even greater clout. One of the most significant contributions of the new amendments was its emphasis upon staff training, an issue uppermost in the minds of parents. In fact, states were held to a higher standard than previously, "whereby they [now had to] *ensure* that those who provide services for students with disabilities (professionals and para-professionals alike) had an adequate knowledge base and the skills" (Twachtman-Cullen, 2000a, p. ix) necessary to meet the needs of these students. The inclusion of paraprofession-als (paras) in the training loop was a great victory for parents, many of whom complained bitterly that the person closest to their children (i.e., the para) was the one with the least amount of knowledge and training!

On the surface, it appeared that "everything was coming up roses" for students with disabilities. After all, the list of *requirements* for schools under *IDEA* read like a parents' "wish list." Some of the more important ones include the following: *related services; supplementary aids and services; assistive technology support; transition planning* for students 14 or older; and *accommodations/modifications,* if needed. Beneath the surface, however, the picture wasn't nearly as rosy as it appeared, given that the "requirements" were not always forthcoming.

For one thing, for many parents the IEP process was a frightening and intimidating experience, and in many cases, more often *hierarchical* than *collaborative.* This occurred because parents weren't always granted the *equal partner* sta-tus that the law afforded them. For another, parents and educators often found themselves on different wavelengths relative to important issues. This was particularly apparent regarding the standard of *appropriateness.* Typically, schools looked upon appropriateness as a *minimal,* court-sanctioned standard. Parents, however, found the school's minimalist position unacceptable, if not downright distasteful, preferring instead that schools *maximize* their children's education.

Needless to say, the different perspectives did little to set the stage for collaboration between parents and the school.

The Not-So-Remarkable Present

That brings us to the present, where in some ways, the more things changed, the more they stayed the same! Take, for example, the elusive concept of *appropriateness*. Notwithstanding that the issue was allegedly "definitively" settled in a 1982 precedent setting Supreme Court case, if the truth be known, today appropriateness is still often "in the eye of the beholder," or at least in the mouth of he or she who makes the most eloquent argument in an emotionally charged IEP meeting or due process case. Clearly, in many parents' minds the issue regarding appropriateness is anything but resolved.

Similarly, over the years the concept of *least restrictive environment* (*LRE*) has, in some quarters, become synonymous with the mainstream, even though the law is clear that the individual needs of the child supercede *IDEA's preference* for inclusive settings. Notwithstanding, many school districts throughout the United States have literally abandoned their self-contained special education settings in their single-minded mission to mainstream *all* children with disabilities, *regardless of individual need*.

What is most ironic about the present-day situation, however, is that as the special education requirements within *IDEA* have become more stringent, the IEP has become less rigorous. In fact, it seems to have taken on the catch phrase of the day in American society—*whatever!* In other words, as society's standards have become looser and more casual, so too have those of the IEP. Twachtman-Cullen (2001) provides the following historical perspective:

> Heretofore, carefully designed annual goals often gave way to goals that were so global that they more

appropriately qualified as *lifetime* rather than *annual.* Likewise, crisply worded instructional objectives followed suit, becoming less definitive and more nebulous. The latter had a negative impact on data specification (and collection!). For example, data for more and more objectives were marked by such non-sensical "measurement" as, *Student will complete an art project with 90% accuracy.* Indeed, to make this type of judgment would be an art form in and of itself! Present levels of performance, the baseline for judging specific progress, was given such short shrift as to be, in some cases reduced to a mere shadow of its former self. In many instances, the conditions for performance didn't even fare as well as that, having been dropped altogether (p.116).

This is consumately unacceptable when one considers that the IEP is the driving force behind individualized educational programming, and the mechanism for effective service delivery.

Before the IEP becomes further watered-down, it is imperative that parents and school personnel alike take a hard look at how well their current IEPs measure up to the letter and spirit of the law that gave birth to *individualized* education. The remaining chapters in this section of the book are devoted to the quality indicators that serve as the standards for judgment.

Chapter 2

Present Levels of Performance

Requirement under *IDEA*

A statement of the child's present levels of educational performance including:

- how the child's disability affects the child's involvement and progress in the general curriculum; or
- for preschool children, as appropriate, how the disability affects the child's participation in appropriate activities;

20 U.S.C. § 1414 (d)(1) (A) (i) (I) (II)

The importance of the statement regarding present levels of educational performance in the IEP cannot be overstated given that,

- *It forms the basis for generating annual goals and objectives that are specifically individualized to the student's needs;* and,
- *It serves as the standard against which to measure performance/progress.*

Ironically, the present levels of performance (PLP) statement is one of the most misunderstood elements of the IEP, and one that is very often neglected. For example, the following "PLPs" are taken directly from an IEP document for an elementary school student with autism:

> **Social-Emotional/Behavioral:** *Has difficulty in this area*

> **Communication:** *Has made progress*

The first thing that needs to be said about the foregoing statements is that neither one addresses the student's *performance!* Hence both are in violation of the *requirement* for such a statement under *IDEA*. Second, neither statement addresses the impact of the student's disability with respect to involvement and progress in the general curriculum, as *required* by *IDEA*. Third, both statements are so unspecific as to be useless in both the judgment of progress and in the generation of individualized goals and objectives.

Sometimes school districts list test scores as the "statement" of present levels of performance. The following is an example of this practice:

> **Academic/Cognitive:** WISC III—V 128; P 111; FS 122

> **Woodcock Johnson:** Reading 84 ss Math: 109 s Writing 93 ss

Despite the air of credibility that quantification imparts, these scores tell us nothing about specific areas of cognitive functioning. Worse yet, they can be quite misleading, given that high IQ scores can give the appearance that all is well, while masking difficulty in such crucial areas of functioning as comprehension, critical thinking, problem solving, executive function, and others.

The Spirit of *IDEA:* What the Law Intends

In order for the statement regarding the student's PLP to be used as the law intended (i.e., as the basis for generating goals and objectives, and as the standard by which to determine progress), certain conditions must be met. Hence, the statement must be, *comprehensive* and *objective* in rendering the following information:

- The student's strengths, specifically tied to what he/she is able to do;

- The student's weaknesses, specifically tied to the *priority* educational needs for the coming year;

- A statement regarding how the student's disability affects his/her involvement and progress in the general curriculum, (or for preschool children, how it affects his/her involvement in appropriate activities); and,

- The source(s) upon which the statement regarding present levels of performance is based (Florida Department of Education, 2000).

A closer look at the above-noted components is in order.

The Student's Strengths Vis-à-vis What He/She Can Do

The focus here is on *current* functioning; that is, how the student's strengths affect what he/she is able to do within the various domains listed in the IEP. It should be obvious that in order for the PLP to serve as the basis for goals and objectives, as well as the standard for determining progress, it needs to be sufficiently comprehensive and detailed to perform these important functions. For example, the following PLP for *Academic Development* falls far short of the mark on both counts: *Student has moderate academic deficits that adversely affect his educational performance.* It should be noted that, in the IEP from which this PLP was taken,

Academic Development is the umbrella category for the following subject areas: *reading, social studies, math,* and *science.* Clearly, the above-noted PLP not only says nothing about the student's performance in each of these areas, but also fails to address the issue of involvement and/or progress in the general curriculum.

The issue of whether to write one comprehensive, all-inclusive description of the student's current status, or separate descriptions for each domain, is left to the discretion of the IEP team. We personally favor separate descriptions, since they relate more directly to the particular domain for which the goals and objectives are to be written, and they are clearer and easier to follow. Hence, in terms of the example given above, we recommend writing PLPs for *reading, social studies, math,* and/or *science,* rather than one global one for *Academic Development.*

The Student's Weaknesses Stated in Terms of *Priority* Educational Needs

The goal here is to specify the student's weaknesses/needs that will be addressed within the goals and objectives for the period covered by the IEP. Two issues are of importance here. The first is that *the needs specified in the PLP must eventually be linked to the goals and objectives that are written to address them.* This would seem to be an obvious point; however, the following example from a student's IEP clearly reveals an all-too-common disconnect:

> **Present Level of Performance:** *Student continues to need verbal and gestural support to move through a conflict or change his expectations.*
>
> **Annual Goal:** *Student will increase his pro-social behavior.*
>
> **Objective:** *Student will be comfortable in simple social situations (e.g., lunch at school).*

Clearly, neither the goal nor the objective follows from the PLP, even though the PLP will be used as the standard for determining progress.

The important second issue regarding the statement of student needs in the PLP, is that it be "pruned" to reflect the educational *priorities* for the period covered by the IEP, since realistically one can hope to accomplish only so much in a given period of time. Without this prioritizing, there is likely to be a "Jack of all trades, master of none" effect, whereby too much is attempted and too little is accomplished. Unfortunately, determining educational priorities is more of an art form than a scientific endeavor.

Involvement in the General Curriculum

This component of the PLP addresses the *impact* of the student's disability on his/her life, particularly as it relates to the student's ability to benefit from the mainstream environment. Issues related to independence, prompt levels, and the general need for assistance in inclusive situations are appropriately stated here. Moreover, information regarding these issues provides the basis for determining not only whether modifications and accommodations are needed, but also the specific types that may be necessary. Despite the importance of these issues, impact statements regarding involvement and progress in the general curriculum, or in appropriate activities for preschool children, are found wanting, or sadly lacking, in many of today's IEPs. To avoid this problem, it is recommended that the concluding statement of the PLP directly address the impact of the student's disability on mainstream functioning. This need not be anything more complex than the following: *Sabrina's executive function deficits impact her ability to function in mainstream educational settings that are not highly structured, or that do not regularly employ visual supports to accompany auditory information.*

11

The Source(s) of Information

Information for the PLP can, and should be based on a *variety* of sources ranging from formal, when possible, and informal assessments, teacher/clinician observation, student performance data, and parent input. The preference for multiple sources of information is based upon the "two heads are better than one" philosophy. It should be noted, however, that *blanket statements, without attribution, hold no one accountable for the judgments rendered.* Conversely, statements that begin with words such as *reportedly, based upon,* or *according to* not only link judgments to their sources, but also go a long way toward rooting those judgments in relevant data. The following PLP for executive functioning takes into account all of the information included within this chapter. The student is a 7th grade boy with ASD.

> *John is able to manage his time and personal belongings with the use of visual supports, including timers and organizational checklists. Likewise, transitions from one activity to another, or from class to class are accomplished with greater ease if transition markers are used. While John is resistant to the use of these supports, several of his teachers have observed that without them, he functions less competently. Parents concur with this judgment, noting that John also has a great deal of difficulty managing his homework assignments. As a result of his disability, John has difficulty keeping up with his mainstream classmates without the use of supports for his executive function deficits. Hence, he needs to develop greater independence in their use to compensate for his organizational problems.*

While it is not within the purview of this particular chapter to consider the appropriate goal and objectives for the above-noted PLP, it should nonetheless be obvious that the goal would relate to the area of executive functioning, and that the objectives would include attention to:

- Developing greater independence in the use of supports to manage school assignments;
- Homework support;
- Developing greater independence in the use of supports for organizational difficulty; and
- Assistance with transitions.

To summarize, when the PLP for a particular domain is well-stated and comprehensive, it not only leads the IEP team down the right path in the generation of goals and objectives, but also provides a suitable standard against which to measure student performance and progress. In other words, it meets both the letter and the *spirit* of the law by doing the job it was intended to do!

Chapter 3

The Underlying Conditions Governing Performance

Performance never occurs in a vacuum. Whether the achievement is a climb to the top of Mount Everest or the safe completion of a tugboat trip, there are unstated, but important factors (i.e., conditions) that govern success. In other words, performance is *always* contingent upon certain conditions, whether or not they are explicitly stated.

Exactly what is it that makes performance conditional? In the Mount Everest example, performance is tempered by many things, including the needs of the climber in the rarefied atmosphere at the top of the mountain, as well as the weather conditions. In other words, without the proper *conditions* (i.e., a supply of oxygen and adequate weather), *performance* (i.e., climbing to the top of Mount Everest) would not be possible. Likewise, in the tugboat example, the safe passage is conditioned upon several factors ranging from the ability of the pilot, to the integrity of the tugboat and the suitability of weather conditions. Short-term objectives

15

for these two activities might be stated, respectively, as follows:

Given a supply of oxygen and adequate weather conditions, Mr. Smith will climb to the top of Mount Everest; and,

Given appropriate pilot training, a mechanically sound vessel, and adequate weather conditions, Captain Doe will navigate safely from point A to point B.

The Link Between Underlying Conditions and Performance

These examples illustrate two important points about underlying conditions. The first is that they can either "make or break" performance. As such, they are powerful contributors to, or if inappropriate, detractors from successful performance. The second is that the underlying conditions relate to what the performer *needs* in order to accomplish the task. Simply stated, *performance that is eminently possible under appropriate (i.e., supportive) conditions may be severely compromised or completely lacking in the absence of those conditions.* At the risk of stating the obvious (but knowing full well that the "obvious" isn't always common practice!), *student success, or the lack thereof, is very much a function of the appropriateness, or lack thereof, of the underlying conditions.*

While it is true that the underlying conditions for the types of activities noted in the examples above are so obvious that they really can go without saying and still be addressed, specification of the underlying conditions governing performance looms particularly large for students with ASD, given their unique needs for certain types of support (i.e., conditions) in order to achieve success. In fact, *we consider the statement of underlying conditions within the IEP to be essential not only to providing successful programming, but also to avoiding inappropriate programming.*

16

Consider the following objective written for a preschool child with Asperger syndrome who, despite repeated reminders to raise his hand, interrupts the teacher constantly in morning circle: *Jimmy will raise his hand when he has something to say in morning circle.* The lack of an underlying condition for performance leaves much to be desired (possibly even the successful accomplishment of the objective!). Specifically, if the teacher uses only verbal reminders, chances are that both she and Jimmy will experience a good deal of frustration, albeit for vastly different reasons. The basis for this is that *verbal reminders alone are insufficient to mediate Jimmy's impulsivity,* since it is a by-product of the compromised executive function system that is associated with ASD. With the appropriate underlying condition, however, the objective is eminently accomplishable, not to mention consummately clear to anyone who sets about to work on it. Thus, *Given a visual cue with a picture of a child raising his hand, Jimmy will raise his hand when he has something to say in morning circle.* The addition of the underlying condition (i.e., visual cue with the picture of the child raising his hand) gives the student a stable and meaningful prompt—an executive function prop, if you will—to remind him of the need to raise his hand. Moreover, it not only gives anyone working on the objective a clear idea of the type of support needed to enable performance, but also ensures *consistency* in the manner in which the objective is addressed across staff. *Clarity of purpose and consistency are two important "cogs" in the "wheel" of successful accomplishment of any and all objectives.*

An *Underlying Condition* for Teachers and Clinicians

Of course, providing support to compensate for Jimmy's impaired executive function (EF) system in the form of a stable visual cue, implies *knowledge* of the following:

• That the student with ASD has EF difficulty; and,

• That his performance is contingent upon this type of visual support.

Despite the crucial importance of this type of knowledge, it is not exactly commonplace. That said, at this juncture, we'd like to set forth a theme that will be echoed many times in the chapters that follow: *The first, most basic building block of appropriate IEP development and effective service delivery is knowledge of ASD and the way in which it affects the particular student who manifests it.* Hence, we'd like to propose an *underlying condition* to govern the performance of teachers and clinicians:

> *Given adequate knowledge of the strengths, weaknesses, and needs of students with ASD,*
>
> **the teacher/clinician will make suitable educational decisions, on their behalf, across a variety of areas and domains that lead to service delivery that is both appropriate and effective.**

Simply stated, without adequate knowledge of both ASD and the way it affects a particular student, it is impossible to determine the strategies, supports, or conditions that are helpful, let alone inimical, to the student.

Unfortunately, it is well beyond the scope of this book to provide specific, in-depth knowledge of ASD. There are, however, many excellent books and articles on the subject of autism and related disorders that can provide high-quality information on the subject. Many of these are listed in *Appendix B.* We single out one of these resources here, given that it was expressly written to provide precisely the type of information that school personnel need in order to understand and program for students with ASD (and also because we are intimately familiar with its contents!). The text—*How To Be A Para Pro: A Comprehensive Training Manual For Paraprofessionals*—contains a 60-page, user-friendly "short course" on autism spectrum disorders covering the following issues: *student placement on the autism continuum; social behavior; communication/language; restricted interests/atypicalities in imagination; sensory issues;* and *theory of mind, information processing,* and *executive function.* The manual also contains reproducible forms for obtaining behavioral and other information, as well as myriad recommendations and supports for addressing a variety of problem situations. Perhaps most important, *How To Be A Para Pro* contains precisely the amount and type of information that is appropriate for regular and special educators alike, as well as clinical support staff and parents as they work together to develop appropriate IEPs for students with ASD.

Ultimately, the choice of reading material rests with the reader, as does the need to render *informed support* to the student with ASD. As noted above, while it is not our intention to offer detailed information on ASD within these pages, the reader will nonetheless find useful information in this regard in Part 2 of the book. The reader is cautioned, however, that we do not consider the material provided in this book to be a substitute for seeking additional, more comprehensive information, elsewhere.

Underlying Conditions and the IEP

From the information provided thus far, it should be obvious that *leaving the underlying conditions to chance is unacceptable.* Hence, it is imperative that they be specified for each objective on the IEP. This will ensure that all objectives are being implemented in a consistent manner in the event of staff and/or programmatic change. Another reason why it is important to clearly articulate the underlying condition is that in some cases successful accomplishment of the objective is actually contingent upon it. Consider the following objective:

> *Jamie will complete a multi-step art project with a maximum of 3 reminders from staff.*

Anyone with knowledge of autism would know that this objective, as written, would have a slim chance for success, given the EF deficits that are inherent in ASD, and the consequent supports required for performance. When the appropriate underlying condition is added, however, the task becomes manageable, and student success, probable:

> *Given a visual template depicting the sequence of activities, Jamie will complete a multi-step art project with a maximum of 3 reminders from staff.*

It should be obvious that, in this case, it is the underlying condition that actually makes the objective achievable. Moreover, it serves to provide information to less knowledgeable staff regarding the types of EF supports needed to scaffold performance and accomplish the objective. This not only enables consistency among school personnel working on the objective, but also generalization across people and settings.

Variations on the Specification of Underlying Conditions

Underlying conditions are typically specified in the first clause of the objective, so as to emphasize what needs to occur *before* performance is to be expected. Specific examples of some common underlying condition clauses will be given later in this chapter. It should also be noted that most IEP forms also contain special sections where team members may specify accommodations and/or modifications. When specified, accommodations and modifications may be considered special types of underlying conditions, given that they delineate what the student needs in order to be successful. For example, if a Nerf® ball is to be used as an accommodation for softball or tennis in adaptive physical education, its use constitutes the condition under which performance in the particular sport is to be accomplished. For additional information on the role of accommodations and modifications for students with ASD, the reader is directed to Chapter 9.

Underlying Conditions vs. Methodology

At this juncture some clarification is warranted, since there can be a good deal of overlap between underlying conditions and methodology. Indeed, oftentimes the line that distinguishes these two concepts is blurry, at best. For example, a particular *methodology* (e.g., the use of *Social Stories)* (Gray, 1994/2000), may also serve as a *condition* governing student performance. In the language of *Social Stories, this is okay*, because in the words of William Shakespeare, "a rose by any other name would smell as sweet!" In other words, call it what you will—*methodology* or *underlying condition*—what matters is that the bases are covered. That said, there may be times when distinguishing between methodology and underlying conditions is deemed advantageous. When that is the case, the following example illustrates one way to distinguish between these interrelated concepts. In Chapter 4 we will discuss another.

It may be useful to think of methodology as coming into play when one seeks to "fix" or remediate a deficit. Underlying conditions, on the other hand, may be thought of as compensatory strategies to circumvent the deficit area. The following example is offered to illustrate the difference between the two terms vis-à-vis the concepts of *remediation* and *compensation*. Myopic or near-sighted individuals have difficulty seeing objects that are far away. Many individuals with this condition compensate for their visual problems by wearing eyeglasses or contact lenses. These prosthetic devices are analogous to underlying conditions, as they compensate for the near-sightedness, and enable successful performance. It is important to note that the individual's *visual acuity* does not change, even though his or her visual *performance* does, in fact, improve. In recent years, medical technology has introduced laser vision correction. If used, it would serve as the *method for correcting/remediating* the condition of near-sightedness.

While this example provides a clear distinction between supports that *compensate* for weaknesses (i.e., underlying conditions), and methods that *remediate* them, real-world distinctions between underlying conditions and methodology are not always clear-cut. So be it! The important point is this: In writing short-term objectives it is important to cover the bases with respect to underlying conditions. If the underlying condition selected overlaps with methodology, think of it as accomplishing two important purposes for the "price" of one! For an in-depth discussion of methodology, see Chapter 4.

Underlying Conditions vs. Prompts

In addition to the foregoing, there is also a good deal of overlap between underlying conditions and prompts. For example, *Given manual signs as cues for verbal expression, Meg will respond appropriately to social exchanges.* It should be obvious that the use of manual signs in this objective serves as both the condition for performance and the prompt that enables it. The following rule of thumb may be helpful in determining when a prompt is also an underlying condition. Since underlying conditions refer to those things that are done *before* a student is expected to perform a task, prompts that are given early-on, as a pre-condition for performance, are likely doing double-duty; that is, serving as underlying conditions, as well. If, however, the prompt is given *after* the student has been preset to succeed by a well-stated underlying condition, it is likely serving as the cue for performance. Hence, the placement of the prompt in the IEP objective (i.e., at the beginning or end of the objective) is often what determines the purpose that it serves; that is, as an underlying condition or as a cue to bring about performance.

Finally, while the fading back of prompts is generally considered desirable, the reader is cautioned against "pulling the rug out from under" students with ASD, by fading back prompts that serve as the *essential underlying conditions* for performance. Indeed, many students with ASD have been ill served when sorely needed visual supports have been faded out of existence. Hence, we urge IEP teams to exercise caution and discretion with respect to this important issue. A complete discussion of prompts and their relationship to student success is presented in Chapter 5.

Examples of Underlying Conditions

The underlying conditions that one selects should be based upon well-established compensatory strategies or other contingencies deemed crucial to student success. Below is a list of some commonly used underlying conditions. It is important to note that this is not a complete list of all of the possible underlying conditions that may be effective for students with ASD. Rather, it is designed to "prompt" the reader to think about the types of conditions that may be necessary for successful performance. We encourage creativity and specificity when determining underlying conditions, on the theory that *well-stated underlying conditions provide the best setup for successful performance.* Below are some common examples:

- *Given visual supports...*
- *Given a visual schedule...*
- *Given a clock that depicts the passage of time visually...*
- *Given direct instruction/teaching...*
- *Given desirable options...*
- *Given opportunities to explore objects in a multi-sensory format...*

- *Given the motivation to do so...*
- *Given repetition...*
- *Given frequent opportunities for practice...*
- *Given a social script...*
- *Given a list of written rules...*
- *Given a model...*
- *Given multi-sensory cues...*
- *Given manual signs...*

To summarize, it should be clear from the information presented in this chapter that when IEP teams write goals and objectives, it is essential that they consider and include those factors that enable successful student performance. Furthermore, underlying conditions should be stated within each objective on the student's IEP. Finally, this chapter also made the important point that adequate knowledge of the features of ASD and how they present in individual students is essential not only to the rendering of *informed* and *appropriate* educational support, but also to overall student success.

Chapter 4

Methodology: Is There a Method to the Madness?

One position to which school districts hold with a tenacity rivaling pit bulls is who determines methodology. Most districts contend that the question lies within their *exclusive* domain. Indeed, this position is so widely held, and so staunchly defended that it is usually accepted as gospel—at least as the *Gospel according to IDEA*! In fact, most school districts consider the subject of methodology to be taboo, and many refuse (albeit politely) even to discuss it at the IEP planning and placement team meeting. Other more accommodating districts will listen to parents' concerns regarding methodology as a courtesy, but ultimately they also reserve their perceived, absolute "right" to decide the issue of methodology on their own. Despite the virtual "institutionalization" of this position, it is nonetheless distinctly incorrect!

The foundation for this bold assertion comes from none other than Reed Martin, J.D., a well-known and well-respected authority on the subject of special education law in the United States. He characterizes as *"dead wrong"* both the position that decisions regarding methodology belong to the schools, and that the subject should not be discussed at IEP meetings. He bases his position on *Board of Education v. Rowley* (1982), the landmark Supreme Court case that addressed special education rights. According to Martin (1996), *quoting from the Court's decision*:

> In regard to the IEP meeting and methodology the Court stated: 'The primary responsibility for formulating the education to be accorded a handicapped child, and for choosing *the educational method most suitable to the child's needs,* was left by the Act to state and local agencies *in cooperation with the parents* or guardian of the child' (p. 44).

He goes on to underscore that it is not only appropriate to *discuss* methodology, but also *incumbent upon the* IEP team to "choose the method **most suitable** to the child's needs" (Martin, 1996, p. 44).

A stronger or more definitive argument for *joint consideration* of methodology is difficult to imagine, especially when one considers that the one advanced above has its roots in statutory interpretation by the United States Supreme Court. How, then, could so many people hold to the view that the school has a preeminent right to determine methodology on its own?

Influences From the Past

The answer to this question is likely rooted in both education tradition and the lack of specificity regarding methodology in the law itself. To be more explicit, since schools were traditionally charged with the mission of educating students, they were also deemed to be the "keepers of the flame" regarding methodology. This stance captured the sentiments of parents at an earlier time in education, whereby they willingly left the business of education to the educators. Clearly, times and traditions have changed, and these changes have been either explicitly or implicitly incorporated into the fabric of *IDEA*. First and foremost, students with significant special needs being welcomed into the public schools is a relatively recent phenomenon. Second, the laws that brought this about have provided a good deal of guidance, heretofore lacking, about the roles of parents and professionals in the education of students with disabilities. Specifically, not only does the law stress *collaboration* between the school and the home, it also grants *equal partner* status to parents in the development of the education plan. Candidly, the very idea of methodology being the sacred cow of the school district—*or of any one party*, for that matter—is antithetical to the collaborative spirit of *IDEA*.

As noted above, another reason for the belief in the school's stronghold on methodology has to do with *IDEA's* lack of specificity on the matter. For example, unlike the specific language governing the present levels of performance cited at the beginning of Chapter 2, there is no *direct* language to cite that specifies the law's stance on the issue of methodology. As a result, *Rowley's* (1982) decision is even more compelling, since the Supreme Court is always the final arbiter in matters where the law is *implicit* or unclear.

Having said that, a word of caution is in order, lest the reader err in the other direction—that of construing the Supreme Court as having granted sole discretion in matters of methodology to parents. This is not the case. What the law does intend, as interpreted in the *Rowley* (1982) case, is for schools and parents to work *collaboratively* to determine the methodology best suited to the student's unique needs. To do so effectively, both parties have to be open-minded, willing to listen, and able to cooperate with one another. *From our perspective it is not so much that home-school collaboration on methodology is a matter of law, but that it is also in the best educational interests of the student, and hence a matter of best practice.* Finally, lest our position be misconstrued, we want to make it eminently clear that, *in no way are we advocating for any specific method or technique, or for the primacy of one party over another.* We are, however, in full support of *collaboration* on what is undoubtedly one of the most important issues in the quest for appropriate service delivery for students with ASD. For more information on specific techniques for collaboration, we refer the reader to *Hopes and Dreams: An IEP Field Guide for Parents and Children with Autism Spectrum Disorders* (Lentz, 2001).

Setting the Record Straight

Despite the fact that the law's intent regarding methodology has been decided by the courts, the issues surrounding methodology are, nonetheless, anything but clear. At the most basic level is the question of what exactly constitutes *methodology?* While on its face the term may appear to be clear, it has been our experience that methodology is often in the eye of the beholder and/or sometimes mistaken for something else. For example, one "man's" methodology may be another "man's" underlying condition, and with good reason for, as noted in Chapter 3, there is a good deal of overlap between the two concepts (a point that will be further elaborated elsewhere).

To ensure that everyone is on the same wavelength regarding this important but nebulous concept, a few definitions are in order. Webster's dictionary defines the term *method* as, "a way of doing something or a procedure for doing something" (p. 628). Similarly, it defines the closely related term *technique* as, "the entire body of procedures and methods..." (p. 1015). The more general term *methodology* is defined as, "a system of methods..." (p. 628). For the purposes of this book we use the terms *methods, techniques,* and *procedures* interchangeably as the discrete components that constitute what is known more generally as *methodology.*

A Means—Ends Proposition

Now that the terms have been defined, it is important to delve into the issue of why careful consideration of methodology is central to the concept of *appropriate* education, and why it is particularly crucial in the case of students with ASD. In terms of appropriate education, one has to look, once again, to the *Rowley* (1982) case. Specifically, the "educational benefit" standard set forth in that case not only has important implications for methodology, but also ties the latter to the concept of an appropriate education. According to the Supreme Court decision rendered in *Rowley* (1982), "Implicit in the congressional purpose of providing access to a 'free appropriate public education' is the requirement that the education to which access is provided be *sufficient to confer some educational benefit* [italics added] upon the handicapped child" (as cited in Wright & Wright, 1999/2000, p. 311). It should be obvious that *inappropriate* methods and techniques would be inimical to the standard of *educational benefit,* and hence a violation of the intent of the law. Furthermore, it is impossible to envision how *inappropriate* means (i.e., methods) could result in *appropriate* ends (i.e., educational benefit).

The enigmatic and unpredictable nature of autism spectrum disorders makes the choice of methodology particularly important. Consequently, teaching methods and procedures that are appropriate for students with other disabilities—or even for other students with ASD—are often distinctly inappropriate for particular students (Peeters & Gillberg, 1999). For example, traditional, hands-on, pre-school activities such as finger painting and working with glue would be off-putting, and hence unsuitable, for a child with ASD who has significant tactile defensiveness. In a similar vein, it is not uncommon to be blinded by the strengths of high-functioning students with ASD, and to *unknowingly* employ teaching methods that actually require them to perform at levels precluded by their disability. For example, more able, hyperlexic, pre-school children with ASD may read (i.e., decode words) at a 3rd or 4th grade level. Blinded by the child's strengths in decoding, and unmindful that hyperlexia, by definition, carries with it problems in *comprehension*, one might *assume* similar ability in reading comprehension where it does not exist. Under this misapprehension, educators could require activities of the child of which he or she is incapable. Likewise, a lack of understanding of ASD in general, or of some of the more subtle symptoms in particular, could cause well-meaning, but unknowledgeable school personnel to use methods and techniques that are actually inimical to the student's best interests. It could also cause school staff to misjudge the student's efforts, and to label him or her as unmotivated or, worse yet, noncompliant.

Examples From the Trenches

The following vignettes, taken from actual case files, are offered to illustrate how easy it is to misinterpret autistic symptomatology and, as night follows day, to then employ inappropriate methods and procedures based upon the misapprehension. Hopefully, the vignettes will also serve to draw attention to the deleterious effect that a lack of knowledge has on both the selection of methodology, and on student outcomes.

Vignette 1:

Susan is a 6th grade student with high-functioning autism (HFA). While she is able to answer questions from her reading book that are concrete and factual, she has a great deal of difficulty answering questions that require her to infer from the information given, that which is not immediately available within the text. Determining that the area of inference-making constitutes a priority educational need, Susan's IEP team developed the following short-term objective:

Given grade-level reading material, Susan will make inferences based upon the circumstances in the stories.

Despite the clearly stated underlying condition, and the straightforward student outcome, Susan made virtually no progress on this objective in an entire year. She also experienced a good deal of frustration with respect to it. An examination of the methods that the teacher was using with Susan is instructive here. Instead of providing her with lower-level more "concrete" inferences as a starting place (e.g., "Why did John take the book out of the library?"), and then having her select the correct answer within a multiple choice format, Susan's teacher jumped straight to the top of the inference hierarchy by selecting those having to do with mental states (e.g., "How did Mary *feel* when her mother told her she couldn't buy a new dress?"). She then required Susan to answer the question as it was presented orally, without the benefit of the less challenging multiple choice format.

This example illustrates how student performance can be compromised by inappropriate methodology—in this case inappropriate vis-à-vis both the level of performance (i.e., beginning at the top of the "inference heap"), and type of response required (i.e., requiring the student to *generate* a response, rather than *select* one from options presented). It also illustrates how a lack of knowledge regarding ASD can jeopardize educational outcomes. In this example, the lack of knowledge is evident on two fronts. First, the underlying condition *assumes* that inference-making is related to grade level, and second, the choice of the particular inferential material would seem to indicate a lack of understanding regarding the role of theory of mind deficits in ASD. Finally, it should be apparent from this vignette that a lack of knowledge of ASD sets up a kind of domino effect, whereby inappropriate methods lead to unsuccessful outcomes.

Vignette 2:

Lucy is a pre-school child with moderate to severe autism who cannot tolerate morning circle for more than 3-5 minutes at a time, without engaging in highly disruptive tantrums. The IEP team has determined that a priority educational need for Lucy is to increase her ability to tolerate morning circle without disrupting the teacher or her classmates. They generated the following short-term objective:

> *Lucy will be able to stay in morning circle for 10 minutes without disrupting her classmates or teacher.*

The lack of an underlying condition should serve as a red flag, since there are a number of ways to accomplish something, not all of which are deemed appropriate. In this particular case, Lucy did indeed accomplish the objective, but her "achievement" came at a cost. In order to enable Lucy to remain in the circle activity for the length of time specified, her para—with the blessing of the teacher—allowed Lucy to tune out the activity, and to engage in self-stimulatory behavior in the form of saliva play. The adage, "at what price glory" comes to mind!

Vignette 3:

Mark is a 4th grade student with Asperger syndrome (AS) whose teachers describe him as *irresponsible*. They cite as evidence of this the following: his messy desk, his proclivity for losing things like pens and books, and his "blurting things out" even after several reminders to raise his hand when he has something to say. Homework is usually late or not turned in at all. Based upon this description, the IEP team generated the following short-term objective:

> *Mark will keep track of his belongings, keep his desk neat, and turn in his homework assignments on time—80%*

The description of Mark, in and of itself, reveals a great deal about the knowledge base (or lack thereof!) of the IEP team. Specifically, there is no acknowledgment that any of the behaviors listed are, in fact, classic symptoms of executive function (EF) difficulty, notwithstanding that EF deficits loom large in students with ASD. When school personnel lack this knowledge, they inadvertently place the student with ASD at-risk with respect to being labeled as irresponsible and/or noncompliant—precisely what occurred in this case. Moreover, such an erroneous perspective has a deleterious effect upon the selection of methods and techniques for remediation. Stated succinctly, the lack of knowledge regarding executive dysfunction in this student obscures the need for executive function props (i.e., visual supports) to provide stable cues, prompt appropriate behavior, and promote greater independence. Worse yet, it leads to the harsh judgments noted above, and to the use of *inappropriate* techniques. In Mark's case, instead of using the organizational supports (e.g., checklists, cue cards, timers, etc.), that can lead to improved functioning, Mark's teachers used verbal reminders (many of which occurred after the fact), so that he had to rely on his impaired working memory (another deficit of the EF system) for guidance! Finally, one is struck by the ambitiousness of the objective, both in terms of the number of behaviors targeted, and the high percentage level set.

These examples illustrate the educational havoc wreaked by inappropriate methodology, not only in terms of student performance and progress, but also in terms of student well-being. It should also be apparent that the thread of commonality running through all of these vignettes, and through the examples given previously, is that *when there is a lack of knowledge or understanding of ASD, there is also concomitant difficulty selecting appropriate methodology for these students.* The importance of this point cannot be overstated, for there are twists and turns along the autism continuum that make the selection of appropriate methodology more of an art form than a scientific endeavor. As stated previously, we feel strongly that knowledge of autism spectrum disorders is the first, most basic building block of effective service delivery— the wellspring, if you will, of appropriate educational programming. To be sure, there are many teachers and clinicians whose knowledge base is enviable, and whose methods and techniques are beyond reproach. There are also countless others who are simply not with the program when it comes to knowledge of ASD or the appropriate methodology to use with students who manifest the conditions under this rubric. Since this is fundamentally unacceptable, the reader is once again urged to seek out further information regarding this multifaceted and enigmatic condition.

To avoid misunderstanding, and to clarify our position with respect to methodology, we recommend the following:

- That all members of the IEP team have sufficient knowledge and understanding of ASD to select appropriate methodology for the student(s)

- That the idea that methodology is the exclusive domain of any one party—school or parent—be laid to rest

- That there be a frank and open discussion regarding methodology during the IEP meeting, as a back drop for *joint* input and decision making

- That, where feasible, there be a description of the methodology to be used with the student within the IEP document (This can be included within the objectives themselves and/or specified elsewhere. This description need not be detailed or complex, and it should be of sufficient flexibility so as not to tie the hands of the teaching/ clinical staff.)

- That members of the IEP team acknowledge—by the time and attention devoted to methodological considerations— that *effective service delivery can only occur in the presence of appropriate methods and procedures*

Methodology and Underlying Conditions: Additional Areas of Overlap

At the risk of redundancy, we offer additional examples of the similarities and differences between *underlying conditions* and *methodology,* beyond those that were discussed in Chapter 3. Consider, for example, the following: *Given a joint activity snack routine, Michael will request items of his choosing from a group of three food choices.* It should be obvious that the phrase, *given a joint activity snack routine,* is both a condition for performance, (i.e., the appearance of the skill requires this context), and a social-pragmatic technique for learning to *request.* In contrast, consider this example: *Given a board game, Amy will take turns with one partner.* Is the phrase beginning with the word *given* a condition or a statement of methodology? We would characterize it as a condition for performance, rather than as a method for teaching the behavior (i.e., Amy will take turns in a board game activity, rather than in some other context.). We base this opinion on the fact that, while the objective specifies the context in which turn taking will hopefully occur, it is "silent" on the issue of *how* the turn taking behavior will be taught. The operative word here is *how;* that is, *if the phrase beginning with the word "given" specifies information relative to how the skill will be taught, as opposed to simply articulating the conditions under which it will be performed, then it addresses methodology.* The following example includes both the condition for performance, and the method for teaching the turn taking behavior: *Given a board game and direct instruction in the use of a turn marker, Amy will demonstrate the ability to take turns by passing the marker to her partner at the appropriate times.* Clearly, the board game serves as the underlying condition (i.e., context) for performance, and direct instruction in the use of a turn marker (e.g., a small circle marked, *My turn*) serves as the method for teaching the behavior. It should also be apparent that the more specificity there is within the objective, the greater the guidance to the educator/clinician carrying out the objective, and the more comprehensible it is to everyone involved.

To summarize, methodological considerations have enormous significance for students with ASD, as well as momentous implications for the delivery of *appropriate* educational services. *While educators are given some leeway with respect to methodology, they are not given license to be the sole determiners of the methods and techniques to be used to address skill development.* That responsibility is a *joint* one between the parents and the school. Typically, parents are extremely knowledgeable not only about their children's strengths, needs, and preferences, but also about the autism spectrum in general. As such, their input on *all* matters related to their children can be invaluable, and should be an integral part of team decision-making.

Chapter 5

Criteria and Prompt Levels

The law clearly states that IEP goals and objectives must be measurable. That is, the IEP team must be able to determine, and provide progress reports regarding, whether or not the student has achieved his/her objectives and, by extension, the long-term goals to which they correspond. The accomplishment of a given long-term goal can be measured by gains over the student's present level of performance, as well as the student's achievement of the more directly measurable short-term objective(s) that relates to it.

The *criteria* that one sets for the objectives are the specific parameters for measuring the extent to which the objectives have been met. The specification of *prompt levels* is intimately related to the criteria set forth, since they provide the scaffolding for performance. Both of these important elements of the IEP will be discussed in this chapter.

The Determination of Criteria

The term *criteria* has a decidedly *quantitative* ring to it, conjuring up images of numbers and other accouterments of the mathematical world. Such criteria as percentages (e.g., 80%), or number of trials (e.g., 4/5 opportunities), are standard fare in most IEPs. Other criteria, though important, are specified less frequently. These include, for example, the number of times a behavior should be performed (e.g., 5 times per day), or a specific time frame for performance (e.g., for a minimum of 10 minutes). All of these measurements provide different ways of assessing a student's mastery of an objective.

While many objectives readily lend themselves to these standard units of measurement, there are many others that do not. For example, the speech of some more able individuals with ASD may be characterized by inappropriate prosody (e.g., monotone or sing-song intonation). Difficulty in this area is not easy to assess, since prosody is really the end product of many important sub-skills that interact with one another (e.g., rhythm, rate, volume, tone of voice, stress patterns, etc.). Furthermore, the determination of appropriate prosody requires a subjective judgment that is not consistent with quantitative measures such as percentages. Unfortunately, measurement "purists" have often steered clear of writing objectives for behaviors that are not quantifiable. This is akin to throwing out the baby with the bathwater. Indeed, IEP teams should not resist writing goals and objectives for behaviors that do not lend themselves to quantitative analysis. Neither should they write the type of nonsensical criteria illustrated by the following: *Given appropriate visual cues, Blake will use appropriate prosody with 80% accuracy.* Despite the quantitative "ring" that 80% lends to the objective, *accuracy* (whatever that means in this particular case) will undoubtedly be "in the ear of the beholder," and sketchy at that! Moreover, one needs to ask, "*80% of what?*"

How then does the IEP team meet its obligation under *IDEA* to measure student performance when the skill to be measured doesn't lend itself to quantification? One way is to design measurement scales for the "unmeasurable" that will allow the IEP team to determine progress. In the example given regarding prosody, one might design a *qualitative rating scale* that can be used to judge the quality of the student's speech according to specified parameters (e.g., volume, rate, etc.). Qualitative means of evaluation will be addressed later in this chapter and in Chapter 8.

The measurement of multidimensional skills presents a particularly thorny problem. Consider the following:

> *Carrie will safely cross the street 4/5 times.*

The objective, as stated, does not measure functional performance in a meaningful way. To wit, Carrie could meet the objective, yet still meet with disaster on the fifth trial! In addition, the term *safely* is vague. After all, Carrie may be able to cross an empty street without being hurt, even if she doesn't stop to look for oncoming cars. Moreover, this objective does not specify the degree of assistance that the student will need to accomplish the task. While independence is always an important goal, it is advisable to scaffold Carrie's performance by providing the supervision/assistance that she will need in the early stages of skill development. A simple task-analysis (i.e., breaking down the behavior into its components) solves the measurement problem. For example,

> *Given direct teaching, a set of rules for crossing the street safely, and adult supervision, Carrie will:*
>
> *1. Stop at the curb*
>
> *2. Look both ways*
>
> *3. Wait until there are no oncoming cars*
>
> *4. Cross the street in a timely fashion*
>
> *4/5 opportunities in a role-play format, with gradually decreasing cues.*

The four behaviors addressed in this objective constitute both the specific behaviors that will be directly taught, and the means by which the student's progress will be measured. This objective also contains other important features. The phrase, *gradually decreasing cues* ensures that progress will also be judged by the degree to which the student moves toward independence. In addition, the objective as worded, provides guidance for caregivers by clearly delineating the types of supports that Carrie will need in order to accomplish the objective. Given the specificity of the behaviors being measured and the clearly defined supports for performance, the "4/5 opportunities" criterion no longer comes across as unrealistic or nonsensical. This is particularly true if it is applied across each of the four behaviors listed to determine progress toward the goal.

The foregoing example illustrates two interrelated and important points:

1. In order for criteria to be useful, they must be able to measure gains in student performance in a meaningful way.

2. Sometimes it is necessary to break down multidimensional behavior (i.e., perform a task analysis) in order to measure functional performance in a meaningful way.

Finally, it should be apparent from the foregoing discussion that there are three elements that impact the specification of criteria within an IEP objective:

1. The behaviors to be measured must be *clearly* delineated;

2. The way(s) in which those behaviors will be measured must be specified; and,

3. The level of prompting/support for skill development must be included.

All of these elements must be present for criteria to render an objective *functional*, *meaningful*, and *measurable*.

The Delineation of Behaviors

One of the great mistakes in the writing of IEP objectives is that of *assuming* that others share our intent. The reader is cautioned not to fall into the trap of thinking that the means by which to judge performance are so obvious that all who read the objective will have the same understanding. In reality, this is rarely the case. If strategies and techniques deemed important to skill development are not directly specified, it is likely that different people will use different, perhaps less successful means to elicit behavior and judge student performance. Likewise, if the behavioral portion of the criteria is vague, it is possible that entirely different behavioral targets for judging performance than those intended will be used. Hence, *since consistency is an important aspect of skill development, it is crucial that behaviors be specified, no matter how obvious they may seem.* For example, a student may have an objective to use a visual schedule—a seemingly straightforward task, on its face. A closer look, however, reveals that the act of using a schedule is, in reality, multifaceted. If this isn't taken into account, a great deal could be open to interpretation, if not overlooked. Consider the steps involved in using a visual schedule:

1. Checking the schedule

2. Identifying the activity

3. Moving to the area

4. Getting materials

5. Completing the activity

6. Putting materials away

7. Putting the schedule symbol in an "*all done*" basket or envelope, or crossing off the completed activity

8. Returning to Step 1

It is important for the IEP team to determine which behaviors are important to the student's completion of the objective. For example, one wouldn't expect a 3-year-old child to obtain the materials needed for an art project, particularly since there could be environmental and safety concerns. On the other hand, being able to "chain through" all of the steps listed above would undoubtedly be advantageous for an 18-year-old student with ASD, since this type of independence would be desirable in a work setting.

It is important to note that students may also need different levels of support for different aspects of schedule use. For example, a student may be able to independently check his/her schedule at the end of an activity, but might need cues and redirection to move to the area where the next activity will take place. Similarly, another student may be able to move independently to the appropriate area where the activity will occur in the classroom, but may need additional support to move to activities outside of the classroom. Thus, the caregiver may wish to specify different levels of support for each step that the student is expected to complete in the process of following a visual schedule. It should be apparent that inattention to the component steps in a multifaceted task makes it all too easy to gloss over elements that may be essential to overall performance.

There are an almost infinite number of behaviors that can be targeted as desired outcomes in IEP objectives. Clearly, it is not possible to specify all of them. Notwithstanding, there are some general guidelines for specifying behaviors that may be helpful to the IEP team. Some of these, along with examples, are listed below:

1. When a behavior has several components, list each of the components that will be measured separately. Some examples of multi-component behaviors include:

    ■ Using a visual schedule

    ■ Completing an art project

42

- Writing a story
- Completing activities of daily living (ADLs) (e.g., washing clothes or dishes, vacuuming, making a bed, etc.)
- Self-care skills (e.g., toileting, brushing teeth, dressing, etc.)
- Buying an item at a store
- Going to a restaurant
- Crossing a street
- Having a conversation
- Solving a problem

2. When several levels of performance are possible within a skill, clarify intent by specifying the level at which the student is expected to perform, as noted parenthetically in the following:

- Following directions (1-step vs. 2- step, etc.)
- Understanding concepts (core vs. concrete vs. abstract)
- Imitating sounds (within the student's repertoire vs. new sounds)
- Communicating (For what purpose(s)?)
- Making a request (What means will be used?)
- Comprehend a written passage (How complex is the passage? What type of comprehension questions will be asked?)
- Writing (handwriting shapes vs. writing one's name vs. writing longer passages; print vs. cursive; What standards are in place for accuracy and neatness?)

Careful consideration of the foregoing will go a long way toward ensuring that the behaviors important to student performance are sufficiently delineated. Furthermore, going through this process also helps to ensure that all staff working on the particular objective will use the same standards for both eliciting behavior and judging student performance.

The Numbers Game: How Will the Behavior(s) Be Measured?

While the topic of *measurement* is discussed at length in Chapter 8, a few points are nonetheless in order here. Once the desired student behavior(s) is clearly specified, the next step is determining how that behavior will be measured. There are many options available to IEP teams. The first step in determining the most appropriate option in a given situation is to determine the manner in which the behavior should be expressed. Once this is done, a criterion that is functionally relevant to the behavior can be assigned. For example, if the behavior is "trial-based" (i.e., the student is expected to perform the behavior a specific number of times), the following means can be used to define criteria:

- Percentage (e.g., 80% of trials)

- Fraction (e.g., 4/5 opportunities)

- Specific number (e.g., 5 times per day)

For other behaviors, specifying explicit time periods may be more appropriate. Consider the following time-based measurements:

- Specific amount of time (e.g., for a minimum of 10 minutes; within 5 seconds, etc.)

- Time fraction (e.g., 5 minutes per hour; 4 times per school day, etc.)

In still other instances, *quantitative* measurement may need to give way to *qualitative* indicators of progress. Consider the following:

- Rating or Likert scales (typically based on ratings from 1–5) that specify a qualitative level of performance. These can be used to judge:

- Qualitative speech measures such as:
  - Prosody
  - Intelligibility
  - Quality of oral motor movements for feeding or speech
  - Quality of problem solving
  - Appropriateness of behavior (e.g., affect)
  - Adherence to a set of rules (e.g., conversational maxims)
- Narrative description

Whatever form of measurement is used, it is crucial that performance expectations be realistic, and that the criteria for judging progress relate to meaningful and functionally relevant performance gains. Creativity and common sense are key elements in making these determinations.

The Specification of Prompt Levels

Most parents and professionals would agree that successful student performance is not only rooted in the appearance of a particular skill, but also in the degree to which the student is able to perform that skill *independently.* Indeed, functional relevance demands independent performance. Independence is a fairly easy commodity to come by when working with neurotypical students. In many ways, these students appear to be driven toward independence, as evidenced by the well-known declaration typical of normally developing 2-year-olds to *"Do it by myself!"* Even children with special needs other than ASD demonstrate relatively flexible learning patterns that enable them to move more easily toward independence. Although learning occurs at a slower rate, many of these students progress from being dependent upon teachers and/or other caregivers, to functioning fairly independently in much the same way as do their neurotypical classmates. One does not see this drive toward independence in students with ASD. In fact, one sees quite the opposite. Specifically, one sees a tendency toward *prompt dependence* (i.e., an inordinate reliance upon specific cues and prompts for performance).

Indeed, skill development in students with ASD has more of a *contingent* quality to it; that is, the ability to perform a particular skill is often a function of certain conditions. Hence, in addition to the underlying conditions discussed in Chapter 3, another "condition" important to consider is the degree to which the student is able to perform the task or skill *independently*; that is, without the assistance of a prompt or cue from an adult or peer.

When a student is unable to perform a task without the assistance of specific prompts or cues, he or she is said to be *prompt dependent*. Over the years, this term has become nearly synonymous with the spectrum of autism (Carr & Kologinsky, 1983; Rincover & Koegel, 1975; Woods, 1987). Specifically, many individuals on the autism spectrum possess skills that they cannot perform in the absence of cues/prompts, even though the latter may be very subtle.

When IEP objectives do not specify prompt levels, adults may use varying levels of cueing to attempt to elicit target behaviors. Such inconsistency can wreak havoc on the performance of students with ASD. In addition, a lack of attention to prompt levels can set the stage for prompt dependency and learned helplessness, both of which are the natural enemies of independent functioning. Indeed, *learned helplessness* may be considered the "final stage" of prompt dependence where performance is quite literally impossible without a prompt or cue. Hence, the bottom line on this important subject is that *not only must prompt levels be specified within the objectives, but there must also be systematic attention to gradually fading back prompts in order to facilitate independence and efficacy within the student.*

Typically, there are several places on the IEP form where prompt levels may be listed. If the IEP format permits, they may also be listed within the body of the objective, as indicated in the examples cited earlier in this chapter. On many forms, however, there is a separate box in which to list the criteria and prompt levels for objectives. The important thing to remember is that, regardless of where they are listed in the IEP document, *prompt levels must never be left to chance!*

A System for Fading Back Prompts

To ensure that prompts are being faded back effectively, a specific *prompt hierarchy* should be specified for each objective or set of objectives appearing under an annual goal. Below is an annotated list of common prompt levels, arranged in order from *independence* to *dependence*:

- *Independent/Initiated:* No prompts are given to the student, since he/she is expected to perform the task independently.

- *Expectant waiting/Expectant time delay:* The adult pauses with a look of expectation to give the student additional time and impetus to respond.

- *Manual sign/Gestural cues:* For the former, the adult uses manual signs such as those in American Sign Language (ASL). For the latter, the adult uses body movements such as:

  - Pointing a finger
  - Shifting one's gaze from student to object/activity
  - Shrugging one's shoulders
  - Moving closer to or farther away from the student
  - Shaking one's head, *No*
  - Nodding one's head, *Yes*

- *Visual Cues:* The student is shown a representational object or picture to cue him/her to perform the behavior.

  > **Note**: Even though we consider *manual signs/gestural cues* and *visual cues* to comprise the *same* prompt level, we separate them here as a convenience to the reader.

- *Verbal cues:* The adult uses his/her voice to cue the student. Examples include:
  - Repetition of directions
  - Verbal instruction (*direct*: "Check your schedule"; *indirect*: "What do you need to do?")
  - Verbal model of language
  - Provision of phonemic/sound cues
  - Cloze sentences
  - Questions

- *Combinations of cues:* At times, a student may need a variety of different cues (e.g., tactile, verbal, gestural, etc.) in order to perform a behavior. These may be referred to as:
  - Multi-sensory cues
  - Tactile and visual cues
  - Visual and verbal cues

- *Physical cues/assistance:* The adult touches the student or physically guides him/her through a desired behavior. (Hand-over-hand assistance constitutes one of the most intrusive types of physical prompts.)

Table 1, *A Prompt Hierarchy*, assigns levels to the prompt categories discussed above, in order to provide the reader with a ready-to-use format for objective writing. In some cases, there may be overlap between or among categories. In others, further individualization in the form of interim steps or additional input may be needed. We leave decisions regarding such individualization to the discretion of the IEP team.

Table 1

A PROMPT HIERARCHY	
Level 0*	Independent Performance / Initiation
Level 1	Expectant Waiting / Expectant Time Delay
Level 2	Manual Signs / Gestures or Visual Cues
Level 3	Verbal Cues
Level 4	Combination of Cues
Level 5	Physical Cues / Assistance

* Level 0 indicates that no prompts are to be used, since independent performance / initiation is required.

Note: To use this prompt hierarchy, select the *lowest* level prompt capable of eliciting the desired behavior, and move toward greater *independence*, keeping in mind that the selection of prompt levels is *always* governed by student performance.

Below are examples of how the information in Table 1 may be applied:

- For objectives that focus on *requesting*, a possible prompt hierarchy might include the following:

  Level 0 Independent/Initiated

  Level 1 Expectant Waiting

  Level 2 Manual Sign Cue ("What?")

  Level 3 Verbal Cue (Question: "What do you want?")

- For objectives that focus on *obtaining attention*, consider the following:

  Level 0 Independent/Initiated

  Level 1 Expectant Waiting

  Level 2 Manual Sign/Gesture (pointing toward arm as cue for student to tap on arm)

  Level 3 Verbal Cue (3rd party prompting student to "tap arm")

  Level 4 Combination of Cues (placing arm next to student and 3rd party prompting to touch arm)

  Level 5 Physical Cue (assisting student to tap adult's arm)

- For objectives that focus on *speech/sound production*, the following prompt hierarchy is offered:

  Level 0 Independent/Initiated

  Level 1 Expectant Waiting

  Level 2 Manual Sign Cue (for word)

  Level 3 Verbal Cue (cloze sentences)

  Level 4 Combination of Cues (tactile and visual)

When a prompt hierarchy is specified in an IEP objective, it delineates how prompts will be faded back to promote independence. For example, a student may be expected to progress from a Level 3 (e.g., verbal cue) to independent performance by the end of the year. There are several ways to document the fading back of prompts. One way is for IEP teams to specify different criteria and prompt levels over the course of a year. Consider the following examples:

- *Six month objective:* 70% consistency, prompt level 3;
  Full year objective: 80% consistency, prompt level 1

- *Six month objective:* 3/5 opportunities given multi-sensory cues;
  Full year objective: 4/5 opportunities given gestural cues

- *Six month objective:* An average rating of 2.5 on a specified rating scale for performance, given verbal and gestural cues;
  Full year objective: An average rating of 3.5 on a specified rating scale for performance, given gestural cues alone

- *Six month objective:* For a minimum of 5 minutes given verbal reminders and visual and gestural cues;
  Full year objective: For a minimum of 5 minutes given a maximum of one gestural cue to complete the activity

Another way to document the fading back of prompts is to write one objective that spans the entire year. The following examples of criteria and prompt levels illustrate how the fading back of prompts may be characterized in a full-year objective:

- 8/10 opportunities per week with gradually decreasing prompts (i.e., verbal cues to gestural cues to expectant waiting to independent performance)

- Within a maximum of 15 minutes given a 50% decrease from baseline level of cues that are needed to complete the task

- A rating scale performance of at least 4, given a progression over time from manual signs to expectant time delay, to spontaneous production of appropriate response

In the foregoing examples, it should be apparent that prompts give useful information regarding both student performance expectations and teaching strategies. Furthermore, they also help to ensure that the adult(s) overseeing the student's programming does not become complacent in maintaining intrusive prompt levels beyond the point that they are necessary.

When is a Prompt More than a Simple Cue?

Sometimes a prompt is *physically* essential to the student's performance. This is often the case in students who present with motor planning difficulty such as *apraxia* or *dyspraxia* (the terms are often used interchangeably). These students sometimes require a prompt to begin a motor sequence. For example, a student may need a phonemic (i.e., sound) cue in order to produce a particular word or sentence. Another student may need to have his/her hands lightly tapped in order to produce the manual sign, *more*. Such prompts should not be viewed in the same way as other cues, as their presence is *physically necessary* for (as opposed to merely supportive of) successful performance, owing to neurologically based motor planning difficulty. These types of prompts may even be considered therapeutic, in the sense of *enabling*, rather than simply *supporting* performance.

Unfortunately, it is not always easy to determine whether a particular prompt or cue is physically necessary to the performance of a skill or task. When this is the case, the student's speech-language pathologist or occupational therapist should be consulted. These individuals can not only help determine whether the student exhibits characteristics of motor planning difficulty, they can also be helpful in providing additional information regarding remediation and the use of appropriate prompts and cues.

It should be noted that, like all prompts, even those that are physically necessary should be faded back gradually, over time, whenever possible. Having said that, the reader is cautioned that the process of fading back physically necessary prompts typically requires additional expertise, as noted above. Hence, this process should be supervised by a certified or licensed speech-language pathologist and/or a registered/licensed occupational therapist.

To summarize, this chapter has addressed the importance of developing functional and meaningful criteria by which to measure objectives. The point was made that since many individuals typically serve the student with ASD, it is crucial that criteria be specific enough to ensure that all caregivers judge performance by the same standards, to ensure consistency. The importance of developing a prompt hierarchy by which to fade back prompts was also stressed.

Chapter 6

The Case for Generalization

Stephen Covey, in his acclaimed book, *The 7 Habits of Highly Effective People* (1989/1990), listed as one of his famous seven habits that it is important to one's success to "begin with the end in mind" (p.95). We attach the same degree of importance to this practice in the delivery of appropriate educational services. While the custom of beginning with the end in mind is a sound one for all students, it is particularly crucial in the case of students with ASD, since the *end* of teaching is not merely the appearance of a particular skill, but rather that elusive "locale" known as *generalization*. The term *generalization* refers to the transference of the acquired skill or skills to other settings, activities, and people. The paucity of attention typically given to generalization activities belies their importance. For example, how functional would it be for a student with ASD to be able to request food items from only his teacher, provided that it was during a snack routine at the horseshoe-shaped table in the classroom? In the world of autism, this example is by no means far-fetched.

As was the case for methodology, *IDEA* does not *directly* address the subject of generalization. Consequently, the issue is open to interpretation. Unfortunately, there is often much resistance to issues that are open to interpretation, as opposed to those that are expressly stated. For this reason, we feel that it is necessary to delve into the reasons why attention to generalization is vitally important for students with ASD. Given our bias in favor of the student, we offer the reader our student-friendly analysis of this important issue.

The Systemic Nature of Generalization Problems in ASD

The term *appropriate education* is defined by statute as one that is "designed... to meet the unique needs of a handicapped child" (20 U.S.C. § 1401 (a) (16). There is a tremendous amount of research documenting the profound generalization needs of students with ASD (Gaylord-Ross, Haring, Breen, & Pitts-Conway, 1984; Gena, Krantz, McClannahan, & Poulson, 1996; Koegel, Koegel, & O'Neill, 1989; Ihrig & Wolchik, 1988; Taylor & Harris, 1995). In fact, problems in generalization are part and parcel of the syndrome of autism (i.e., they are endemic). Moreover, we feel that the generalization needs of students with autism go well beyond those of students with other disabilities. While we recognize that the latter may also have problems with generalizing information, their difficulties appear to be rooted in more superficial circumstances; that is, in external conditions such as inattention, forgetfulness, distractibility, etc. *Students with ASD, however, have deep-seated, systemic problems with generalization that appear to be "wired in" to the disability.* In other words, there are deficits inherent in the disorder itself that can actually preclude individuals with autism from *independently* "connecting up" disparate pieces of information in order to form a generalized concept. For example, *stimulus overselectivity* is a well recognized feature of autism in which the student over-focuses on idiosyncratic and typically irrelevant stimuli, while ignoring the relevant cues that enable the establishment of meaning. Stimulus overselectivity can interfere with the generalization of skills to an unfamiliar environment if the student, over-focusing on an irrelevant detail, ignores the relevant cues that are intended to prompt the learned behavior in the new environment (e.g., focusing on one small aspect of a picture cue, rather than the gestalt). Similarly, deficits in areas such as executive function and theory of mind can also interfere with the generalization of skills across settings, activities, and people.

It is important to note that generalization difficulty is not confined only to traditional academic subjects, but extends also to such areas of functioning as executive function, communication/language, social skills training, and others. Olley and Stevenson (1989) talk about the serious limitations in social skills progress in preschool children with autism that result from "their failure to generalize" (p. 356). These authors distinguish between the following two different types of generalization:

> Most typically social behavior learned in one setting does not occur in other settings. Skills learned in the presence of certain children or adults are not used in the presence of other people. Behavior learned at one time seems lost or forgotten a short time later if the exact conditions of training are not present. All of these are examples of failures in stimulus generalization. Response generalization is a similar, difficult problem. A student may learn one response and use it consistently, but when a somewhat different response is called for, generalization does not occur (Olley & Stevenson, 1989, p. 356).

Berkell (1992) echoes the sentiments of Olley and Stevenson, and makes a strong case for the link between generalization and learning, "Generalization strategies, including teaching skills across settings, materials, and people, are *crucial to successful instruction"* [italics added] (p. 101). Likewise, Klin and Volkmar (2000), list the following as one of six specifications felt to be "positive and necessary" when judging the *appropriateness* of programming for students with Asperger syndrome:

> An important priority in the program is to foster generalization of learned strategies and social skills.... From a programming perspective what is important is to define generalization explicitly as a goal to be achieved, including the various specific strategies to be implemented and the goals in the light of which the success of the program will be measured (p. 348).

The bottom line with respect to the issue of generalization for students with ASD is that *there is clear research evidence that demonstrates that the success of the student's educational program is directly linked to the degree to which he or she has achieved generalization of acquired skills across settings, people, and activities.* We think that Powers (1992) put it best when he said, "The powerful instructional technologies that have been developed over the years will be of little long-term value to children with autism if skills acquired fail to generalize to untrained environments" (p. 237). Based upon the foregoing, and the fact that students with ASD *require* specific assistance in making the connections that are necessary for generalization to occur, *we believe that generalization strategies and conditions must be expressed within the IEP, and directly addressed, if the goal of appropriateness is to be realized.*

If the information included above is insufficient to convince skeptics of the importance of *direct* attention to generalization, consider the federal court case, *Drew P. v. Clarke County School District* (1989). In that case the lack of generalization of skills from the school environment to the home was cited as a material reason why the child's parents withdrew their son from the public school and placed him in a private residential program for students with autism. The court, applying the *Rowley* (1982) standard, decided in favor of the parents that placement was necessary in order for the student to derive *any* educational benefit.

We have spent a good deal of time on the issue of generalization to make our case, as it were. Our interpretation of how the concept of generalization dovetails with that of *appropriate* education is ours alone. It is based upon what research and clinical practice tell us about the needs of individuals with ASD. While we feel that there is support for our position in case law and within *IDEA* itself, *our arguments in favor of including specific information regarding generalization in the IEP are made on sound educational grounds.* As stated elsewhere in this book, we leave matters related to the law in other more capable hands.

The Nuts and Bolts of Generalization

An all too common mistake that teachers and clinicians make regarding generalization is to treat it, quite literally, as an afterthought (i.e., as something to be thought of *after* the student has acquired a particular skill). In many cases, that is too late. Remember the adage discussed at the beginning of this chapter, "Begin with the end in mind" (Covey, 1989/1990, p.95). Specifically, *given the profound difficulty that students with ASD have with the generalization of skills, it is necessary to begin this time- and labor-intensive process at the beginning of the teaching cycle, rather than at the end.*

While it is beyond the scope of this book to provide detailed "how to" information on generalization, it should be noted that there is a generalization "technology" that has been found to be effective for students with ASD. For more information on the principles of generalization, as well as on specific strategies to promote it, the reader is referred to the work of Stokes and Osnes (1988). For our purposes it is important to highlight four interrelated, general factors of which educators and clinicians need to be mindful as they set about the task of programming for generalization. The first factor is that of *time*. Simply stated, students with ASD need to have a great deal of "time in" regarding skill development across different settings, activities, and people, in order to have sufficient practice vis-à-vis generalization targets. The second factor is that of *structured opportunities*. In other words, mere *exposure* to different settings, activities, and people is not enough. Rather, there must be carefully structured, controlled, and "created" opportunities for the student to exhibit the skill(s) in each targeted circumstance. The final two factors are arguably the most important. Teachers and clinicians not only need to assist students in making the *connections* that they are not able to make for themselves, but also to *scaffold* skill development by providing the necessary supports.

Documenting the Generalization Protocol

There are many ways to include generalization information within the IEP. The most direct way is to include it within the body of the short-term objective. Consider the following:

> *Given direct instruction, manual signs, and a variety of structured situations in which important information is lacking, Sally will obtain information by asking relevant questions, 8/10 times per week, across different people, activities, and settings, with gradually decreasing prompts.*

The environmental setup—*structured situations in which important information is lacking*—requires the teacher or clinician to contrive a variety of situations in which the questioning can take place. This meets the structured opportunity provision discussed above. The 8/10 times per week provides a sufficient level of intensity with respect to "time in" and practice regarding skill development, as well as a means by which performance can be measured. The specification of manual signs helps to scaffold performance, and the reference to decreasing the prompt levels ensures attention to promoting independence. Finally, specification of the generalization targets (i.e., people, activities, and settings) ensures that all-important attention to the transference of skills.

Additional ways of expressing generalization criteria within short-term objectives are as follows:

> *Given direct teaching and visual supports, Stephen will demonstrate comprehension of 6 concrete concepts across a minimum of 3 different settings, activities, and people, each day, with gradually decreasing prompts, at a consistency level of 80%.*

> *Given direct instruction in the use of a story board, Sam will demonstrate an understanding of character and setting by selecting appropriate representations from a group of those presented, 8/10 times, per story, across 6 different stories, and across different people and settings.*

Note: The previous objective does not include information regarding prompt levels, as it was included elsewhere in this student's IEP.

Generalization criteria can also be specified as a "goal" separate and apart from the short-term objective. Consider the following:

> *Given direct instruction/visual cueing, and a variety of situations in which verbal clarification is needed, Louise will use appropriate repair strategies to inform the listener of the need for additional information. (Repair strategies to include: requests for clarification; requests for repetition; and statements indicating a lack of understanding.)*

Generalization Goal: 7–10 structured opportunities for practice will be provided across people, activities, and settings throughout the day.

To summarize, the particular manner in which generalization criteria are expressed (i.e., as part of the short-term objective, or as a separate subset of it), is left to the discretion of the IEP team. Sometimes the question of how to express information is dictated by the IEP form, itself. The important point to be made, however, is that *information regarding generalization must be explicitly expressed in order to ensure attention to this very important element of the IEP.*

Before leaving this topic, it is important to consider the issue of maintenance of skills over time. In our opinion, this topic is intimately related to that of generalization. Specifically, if there is no attention to the generalization of skills whatsoever, and as such they are exhibited in only one activity and setting with one person (e.g., with the speech-language pathologist in the therapy room), how and why would the student maintain them? Conversely, when students with ASD are able to make the connections that signal the need for newly acquired skills across various settings, activities, and people, there is a greater likelihood that the skills will be maintained over time, as they will be more serviceable (i.e., functional) for them. Finally, *in order to make the goal of maintenance of skills over time a reality, we recommend that "mastered" skills be recycled across activities, environments, and people on a regular basis throughout the course of the year.* Further, we recommend that future teachers and clinicians have access to earlier IEPs and documentation of students' progress to ensure that previously acquired skills are mastered as new skills are being learned.

Chapter 7

Goals and Objectives:
The Heart and Soul of the IEP

Requirement under *IDEA*

(ii) a statement of measurable annual goals, including benchmarks or short-term objectives, related to:

- (I) meeting the child's needs that result from the child's disability to enable the child to be involved in and progress in the general curriculum; and

- (II) meeting each of the child's other educational needs that result from the child's disability;

20 U.S.C. § 1414 (d) (1) (A) (ii) (I) (II)

Lest the reader wonder why we have waited until the seventh chapter of this book to finally get to the "heart and soul" of the matter, please rest assured that we have done so by specific design and with an important purpose in mind. Specifically, it is our contention that the annual goals and short-term objectives or benchmarks are so vital to the success of the student's educational program that their consideration should come only *after* the IEP team has carefully considered the factors that are integral to their successful accomplishment. Toward this end, in the foregoing chapters we have discussed the crucial, preliminary building blocks of IEP development that are of central importance in the construction of need-based, appropriate goals and objectives. These *essential elements of the IEP* are: *present levels of performance; underlying conditions; methodology; prompt levels and criteria for performance;* and *generalization.* We are now ready to apply the information gleaned in the foregoing chapters to the writing of annual goals and short-term objectives or benchmarks. Before we do so, however, it is necessary to address the distinction between short-term objectives and benchmarks, and to define, and distinguish between goals and objectives, as well. We will also consider the many pitfalls involved in the writing of instructional objectives.

The Distinction Between Short-Term Objectives and Benchmarks

Reed Martin, J.D., (n.d.) refers to *short-term objectives* as the "measurable intermediate steps," and to *benchmarks* as the "major milestones" by which to measure progress toward the achievement of the annual goal. According to Martin (n.d.),

> Generally, benchmarks establish expected performance levels that allow for regular checks of progress that coincide with the reporting periods for informing parents of their child's progress toward achieving the annuals goals. An IEP team may use either short-term objectives or benchmarks or a combination of the two depending on the nature of the annual goals and the

needs of the child (Part I, Measurable Annual Goals section, para. 4).

The overlap between objectives and benchmarks should be obvious. According to the Florida Department of Education (2000),

> Benchmarks and short-term objectives are similar in the following ways:
>
> - They provide a map or path the student will take to attain the annual goal.
> - They link the preset level of educational performance and the annual goal.
> - They guide the development of effective and relevant modifications and strategies (p. 50).

For the sake of convenience, and to avoid unwieldy language, we will confine ourselves to the discussion of short-term objectives, per se. Notwithstanding, the reader is asked to consider *benchmarks* as the "silent partner" in this discussion, deserving of equal care and consideration within the IEP document, whenever their use is preferred over that of short-term objectives.

Goals and Objectives: Commonalities, Distinctions, and Perplexities

Webster's College Dictionary defines the word *goal* as, "the result or achievement toward which effort is directed; aim; end" (p. 571). *Objective* is defined as, "something that one's efforts or actions are intended to attain or accomplish; purpose; goal" (p. 933). Synonyms for both words are virtually identical. How then can they be distinguished? Lawrence M. Siegel, in his book *The Complete IEP Guide: How to Advocate for Your Special Ed Child* (2001) looks at goals as broad statements of educational aims for students, and at objectives as "the skills [the] child must master to reach a stated goal"

(p. 9/2). Under the circumstances, given the similarity between the two terms, and in the interest of avoiding redundancy, his distinction is the only one that seems to makes sense.

In addition to the issue of similarity, there is also a good deal of confusion regarding the measurability requirement of goals and objectives laid down by *IDEA*. Some individuals believe that the annual goals have to be stated in distinctly measurable terms. Consider the following annual goal used as an example by the Florida Department of Education (2000) in its manual, *Developing Quality Individual Educational Plans: A Guide for Instructional Personnel and Families:*

> *"Edner will use organizational strategies to improve his ability to complete classroom assignments and function independently by 25% in the regular 6th grade classroom." (p. 246)*

Siegel (2001), an attorney specializing in special education law, does not advocate a stringent measurability standard in the statement of annual goals. Instead, he assigns the measurability provision to the short-term objectives. Consider the following:

> **Goal:** *Tim will improve his reading comprehension.*

> **Objective:** *Tim will read a four-paragraph story and demonstrate 75% comprehension using objective classroom tests.*

> **Goal:** *Jane will improve her writing skills.*

> **Objective:** *Jane will write a three-sentence paragraph with subject and predicate sentences, per teacher evaluation* (Siegel, 2001, p. 9/2).

What's an IEP team to do in the face of two such diverse ways to conceptualize annual goals? We believe that the problem here is one of interpretation. In other words, a *literal* interpretation of the *IDEA* requirement, *"a statement of measurable annual goals, including benchmarks, or short-term objectives…"* can lead one to write goals in narrowly conceived, stringent, measurable terms. When this is done, however, it appears to distort the properties of the goal. In other words, instead of the broad-based umbrella category for the more specific objectives in service to them, the goals themselves take on the properties of objectives. In fact, they become indistinguishable from them.

The question here is not whether to measure or not to measure, but rather where to assign this important task—to the goals or to the objectives. While the issue is at best open to interpretation, and at worst, confusing, *we believe, that the stringent measurability requirements are best left to the short-term objectives.* This interpretation gives the IEP team flexibility to write several detailed objectives to amplify the broader based goal. It also enables the goal to fill a very important function—that of specifying the *educational need* that gives rise to the objectives. Furthermore, *we view narrowly worded goals as needlessly restrictive, and hence more limiting with respect to instruction, overall.* Finally, we believe that properly written objectives with their clearly stated measurement criteria, render the goals from which they issue forth, *measurable* in the ways specified within the objectives themselves. For example, some school districts characteristically use the phrase *as measured by the following objectives,* or similar language, within the body of their goal statements (e.g., *Susan will increase her participation in class as measured by the following short-term objectives.*). The task for the IEP team is to write objectives that will address measurable aspects of Susan's participation in class. This wording has the advantage of linking the accomplishment of the goal to each of the objectives that addresses it. More specific information on measurement and data collection will be the subject of the next chapter.

Putting Goals in Their "Proper" Place

The annual goal in the IEP is the statement of what the team hopes to accomplish in a given year, for a given domain or area of instruction. While it is permissible that it be stated in broader terms than the more narrowly construed objectives, it should not be so broadly based as to qualify as a *lifetime*, rather than *annual* goal! Neither should it be so global or abstract as to be little more than a glittering generality lacking in both form and substance. The following goal illustrates both: *To maximize the development of self-esteem.* Firstly, the *maximization* of self-esteem would seem to be a rather ambitious *annual* goal for a person with autism. Secondly, unless the objectives clearly delineate the overt behaviors that signal the abstract concept *self-esteem,* the IEP team will be hard-pressed to measure whether or not the goal has been accomplished. Thirdly, the word *development* serves as a kind of hedge (both literally and figuratively) behind which it is easy to sound lofty, while actually (albeit inadvertently) evading measurable behavior (i.e., performance). Specifically, how exactly does one measure *development?*

Using "hedge" words is, in reality, a common problem in the statement of annual goals. It stems from confusing *process* with *product/outcome.* The following phrases contain italicized hedge words: *develop* an understanding (or appreciation) of, and *learn* to recognize. Both are process, rather than outcome oriented. Hence, they add unnecessary layers that obfuscate overt performance. In the case of the first phrase, it would be more to the point to say, student will *demonstrate* understanding (rather than devote efforts to the *development* or *appreciation* of understanding). Objectives could then be written that describe the behaviors (i.e., outcomes) that will be accepted as indicative of understanding. Likewise, the second phrase noted above should be re-written as, *student will recognize*—or student will *select*—since these revisions point directly to the desired outcome (i.e., the *act* of identifying something, as opposed to the process of *learning* to do so).

For the reader who is tempted to gloss over goal statements as superfluous, or as less important than the "meatier" short-term objectives—and we have seen evidence of this in many IEPs—consider the following Lewis Carroll quote:

> *"Would you tell me please, which way I ought to go from here?"*
>
> *"That depends on where you want to get to."*
>
> *"I don't care where."*
>
> *"Then it doesn't matter which way you go."*

It is a truism that if you don't know where you are going, it doesn't matter how you get there. The same is true for goals and objectives. Specifically, if you don't have a clear, well-stated goal for instruction (i.e., a statement of what you want to accomplish) you won't know the steps to take to get there (i.e., to achieve it). Simply stated, *if instruction is to be effective, there must be a connection between the need that is stated in the goal, and the nature of the instruction designed to meet the need that is specified in the objective.*

From the Sublime to the Ridiculous: The Saga of Instructional Objectives

In the early days of *IDEA*, known then as *P.L. 94-142*, the writing of instructional objectives was treated with the thought, care, and respect it deserved. Fuzzy language, difficult-to-grasp abstractions, and impossible-to-measure requirements were considered unacceptable. After all, the mid 1970s belonged, in large part, to behaviorism with its emphasis upon *observable* outcomes and *measurable* performance. In those days the *science* of objective writing trumped the *art* of objective writing. As such, with few exceptions, objectives were crisply worded and clearly stated. They also included the conditions for performance, as well as the criteria by which to judge progress. The only real downside to all of this was the "throw the baby out with the bathwater phenomenon." Specifically, in some cases, the rigid adherence to the observable and measurable requirements for behavior led some individuals to disregard the instruction of important material, simply because they weren't able to state objectives for it in observable or measurable terms. Despite this exception, the rule of the day was that typically, objectives said what they meant, and meant what they said!

Now for the ridiculous. The inexorable march to the carefree 1990s, with its "whatever" attitude, led to a watering down of the IEP. The objectives were among the hardest hit. Take for instance the specification of underlying conditions. Once a mainstay of instructional objectives, underlying conditions today are either catch-as-catch-can, or missing altogether from many IEPs. Likewise, there is far less emphasis upon either the observability of behavior or the measurement standards for performance. With respect to the latter, consider the following measurement criterion: *Mark will independently respect other people's needs, rights, and desires when asked—80%.* Even before one ponders what 80% refers to, or how to measure *respect*, the oxymoron (i.e., *independent prompted* performance) renders the objective (and its accomplishment) moot! Unfortunately, when there are inadequate or inappropriate measurement standards for performance (not to mention impossible requirements), there is no accountability for results (or the lack thereof!). In many cases objectives are not even remotely connected to the goals from which they supposedly flow. The following examples of inadequate (ridiculous?) objectives illustrate these points, and a few others:

> ***Goal:*** *Karen will improve social skills to age-appropriate levels.*

> ***Objective:*** *Karen will be able to see or find multiple responses to challenging situations (appropriately).*

Even without being able to decipher the poorly worded objective, it is obvious that there is no relationship between it and the goal it is supposed to address. In addition, *improving social skills to age-appropriate levels* for a girl with autism is too ambitious even to qualify for a lifetime goal, let alone an annual one! Unfortunately, the situation doesn't improve for Karen with the next objective, either:

> **Objective:** *Karen will be able to shift attention from one activity (academic or situation).*

The objective, as worded, is consummately unclear, not to mention barely literate. Moreover, since the ability to shift attention is a function of the executive function system, the objective does not follow from the goal, since it is directed toward improving social skills. Unfortunately, the final objective is about as measurable as "truth, beauty, motherhood, and apple pie," and just as global. To wit,

> **Objective:** *Karen will be able to improve self-confidence and assume leadership.*

Enough said!

Consider the following objective for a 1st grade boy who is scarcely at the one-word stage of language development:

> **Objective:** *In a structured situation with verbal cueing, Ben will use the pronouns he, she, it, and they in sentences—orally.*

In a similar vein, the next one was written for a pre-school boy who is essentially *nonverbal:*

> **Objective:** *Given instruction, Bobby will demonstrate improvement in articulation skills.*

These examples are the instructional equivalents of building a house by starting with the roof. In neither case is there a foundation on which to build anything of value. Finally, this one is about as wishy-washy as an objective can get:

> *Objective:* Rita will be pre-set and exposed to an after-school club activity 1 time/week depending on the club, with support.

Can anyone seriously believe that such drivel (i.e., mere *exposure* possibly once a week to whatever club happens to be available) is what the architects of *IDEA* had in mind when they coined the phrase a *free appropriate public education?* Unfortunately, an entire IEP team must have believed it, because it's one of Rita's objectives for the coming year!

Besides being inept, the foregoing goals and objectives have one other thing in common. Since they were all written for actual, not hypothetical children with ASD, they stand in the way of appropriate educational programming and effective service delivery. We have spent a good deal of time on this subject in the hope of motivating IEP teams to take a hard look at their own IEPs and to ask the following question: *Does this IEP blueprint provide the necessary specifications to enable school staff to build appropriate educational programs, and deliver effective instructional services to students with ASD?* If the answer to this question is not an unqualified *yes,* the information within this book can go a long way toward rectifying the situation. The remaining sections in this chapter deal with the elements that must be present within instructional objectives if they are to qualify as appropriate.

The IEP as a System of Interdependent Components

Webster's College Dictionary defines the term *system* as "an assemblage or combination of things or parts forming a complex or unitary whole" (p. 1356). The applicability of the term to the IEP is irrefutable. Consider the following scenario. Objectives are the vehicles for delineating intended instructional outcomes. Hence, they are the *means* to a very important *end*—appropriate education. As important as objectives are, however, they do not stand alone. In fact, like the skeletal system in which one bone must connect to another for action to occur, so too the component parts of the IEP system must interconnect with, and depend upon one another for appropriate educational "action" to take place. For example,

- *Annual goals* for students are derived on the basis of the priority needs

- expressed in the *present levels of performance,* and

- articulated in the *instructional objectives.*

It should be obvious that if short shrift is given to any one of these important components, the student's entire educational program will be short-changed, as well.

The reader may wonder how objectives relate to methodology. Robert F. Mager, an internationally renowned writer in training and education, and arguably the "guru" of instructional objectives, has this to say about the interrelationship between objectives and methodology, "When clearly defined objectives are lacking, there is no sound basis for the selection of instructional materials and procedures. If you don't know where you're going, how will you know which road to take to get there?" (Mager, 1997b, p. 14). Mager's logic is irrefutable, notwithstanding that the sentiment expressed is chilling, especially when one considers the sorry state of objectives in many IEPs for students with ASD.

Since objectives, by law, have to be measurable, they are also intimately connected to the criteria for performance. According to Mager (1997b), "Without clear objectives it simply isn't possible to decide which measuring instrument will tell you what you want to know" (p. 15). The remainder of this chapter will address the three essential features that define sound objectives, as well as the interrelationships among them.

The "Three Faces" of Properly Executed Objectives

Throughout this book we have used the phrase *effective service delivery,* a phrase that is synonymous with *effective instruction.* While all of the essential elements of the IEP contribute to the effectiveness of instruction, we confine ourselves in this section to the short-term objectives, leaving until the *Epilogue* a more comprehensive discussion of the totality of effective service delivery.

What makes instruction *effective?* The first thing that comes to mind is that for instruction to be effective there must be a change in performance. *If instruction merely maintains the status quo, it can hardly be termed effective.* The second thing that comes to mind, however, is that change can go in either direction; that is, it can result in *desired* gains, or in *undesirable* outcomes. Needless to say, *if instruction results in undesirable ends it is not only ineffective, but also harmful.* There are many ways in which objectives can be harmful. For example, objectives that hold students with ASD to standards that their disability precludes them from attaining lead to frustration and anxiety, both of which are inimical to educational progress/success. In order to avoid ineffective instruction or harmful side effects, it is important to consider the important features that characterize appropriate objectives.

Mager (1997b) points out that for objectives to be appropriate they must be *useful.* He delineates the following standards for determining the usefulness of objectives:

- They must lead one to methodology that enables instruction to be "relevant and successful";
- They must help "to manage the instructional process itself;" and,
- They must lead one to the appropriate means for determining the extent to which instruction has been successful (p. 43).

Mager (1997b) also lists the following three characteristics that must be included *within the body of the objective* if it is to lead to effective instruction:

1. **Performance.** It describes what the learner is expected to be able to DO.

2. **Conditions.** It describes the conditions under which the performance is expected to occur.

3. **Criterion.** It describes the level of competence that must be reached or surpassed (p. 51).

The underlying conditions for performance, as well as the criteria for it, have been discussed, in-depth, in previous chapters, and need not be re-visited here. Suffice it to say that both are intertwined, not only with performance, but also with all of the other essential elements of the IEP. Performance, however, does need further clarification at this juncture.

Two issues relative to performance are particularly crucial. The first, and most obvious, is that *performance means doing*. Hence, if an objective is about the following:

- *Carrying out* an action,

- *Selecting* the main idea, or

- *Writing* a sentence,

the performance is obvious, since all of the italicized words are *performatives* that directly relate to *observable behavior*. That brings us to the second issue—how does one handle performance based upon behavior that cannot be directly observed? As noted elsewhere in this chapter, some individuals have avoided this issue altogether, thus throwing out the proverbial baby with the bathwater. This, however, is unacceptable since the things that human beings value most in life are typically rooted in things that cannot be directly measured (e.g., truthfulness, responsibility, etc.). To dismiss them out of hand simply because they cannot easily be assessed is consummately shortsighted. That said, have we reached an insurmountable impasse where the baby must be thrown out with the bath for the sake of overt performance? Not at all.

Mager (1997a, 1997b) has a simple answer to this dilemma that will undoubtedly serve IEP teams (and students!) well. He uses the term *indicator behavior* to represent actions or activities that can provide *direct* information when the objective is stated in *covert* terms. According to Mager (1997b), "We can write about covert performances in objectives as long as there is a *direct* [italics added] way of finding out whether the performance is in good shape" (p. 77). Note how the following examples of indicator behavior clarify the intent of the covert wording:

Covert Wording: *Discriminate shapes.*

Indicator Behavior: *Sort circles and squares (or triangles and rectangles, etc.).*

Covert Wording: *Understand verbs.*

Indicator Behavior: *Circle (or underline) verbs.*

Finally, the best way to identify indicator behaviors is to ask oneself the question, *What does the student need to do to demonstrate mastery of the objective?* (Mager, 1997a, 1997b). The list that is generated can be used to pinpoint overt performance. Before leaving this topic, it is important to note that there may be times when including the indicator behavior within the body of the objective may be too cumbersome. At these times, *it is acceptable to include the indicator behavior in an explanatory note in close proximity to the objective.* However you choose to do it, the bottom line is: *Indicator behavior needs to be specified somewhere within the IEP document.*

The "Covert" Benefit of Well-Stated Short-Term Objectives

The final topic of this chapter is that of *consistency*, which we characterize as *covert* only in the sense that it seems to simply emerge when the essential elements of the IEP interact to function as the "well-oiled" system it is designed to be. In point of fact, *consistency is the crucial by-product of attention to all of the important details that lead to effective service delivery.* Take, for example, the case of Thomas and the differences between the following two objectives:

> *Thomas will develop an understanding of idioms* vs. *Thomas will select from a group of four possible explanations the item that best describes what the idiom means.*

Which objective of the two given has the better chance of being carried out in a consistent manner across people and activities? The answer to this question is so obvious that it needs no further elaboration here. The point to be made is that when objectives are clearly stated, comprehensive, and understandable, they are more apt to be carried out by a variety of people, across a variety of settings, in the manner intended.

To summarize, the information provided within this chapter is intended to enable the reader to:

- Understand the important distinctions between goals and objectives;
- Look upon the IEP as a systemic document in which all of its elements are interdependent;
- Write indicator behaviors when performance is covert; and,
- Recognize that consistency is a crucial by-product of clearly stated objectives.

If all else fails, perhaps the "recipe" for objective writing set forth by Mager (1997b) will make the all-important task of writing appropriate and useful objectives a little easier:

 a. *Write a statement that describes the main intent or performance expected of the student.*

 b. *If the performance happens to be covert, add an indicator behavior through which the main intent can be detected.*

 c. *Describe relevant or important conditions under which the performance is expected to occur. Add as much description as needed to communicate the intent to others* (p. 107).

Chapter 8

Measurement, Data Collection, and Evaluation

The previous chapter summarized how the essential elements of the IEP may be melded together into effective, functional, and measurable long-term goals and short-term objectives. This chapter serves as a kind of "grand finale" to the process of designing effective IEPs, with its "triple crown" of *measurement, data collection,* and *evaluation*. In this chapter we consider the evaluation of the student's response to teaching methods, task expectations, and prompts/supports, as well as a schedule for evaluation.

Unfortunately, to many professionals, *data* is considered a "four-letter-word!" After all, in this busy world of ours data collection involves time, paperwork, analysis, and interpretation—all of the things most of us would like to avoid. Moreover, many argue (with good reason) that data collection can be intrusive, interfering with the process of teaching, especially when working on functional skills in naturalistic contexts. These problems (i.e., intrusion and interference) are only compounded when one takes data on multiple objectives across many students. When all is said and done, there are those who contend that much of the data collected is meaningless; that is, it is not a true reflection of either student performance or capability. As a result of all of these considerations, data collection is more often than not found wanting in today's IEPs.

Even when school personnel are committed to data collection, it is often performed in a haphazard manner, making it sketchy, at best, and misleading, at worst. Because of the difficulties associated with the collection of data, several important issues will be discussed in the following sections of this chapter, each of which is designed to address a question/concern regarding specific aspects of this important subject.

What is the Purpose of Data Collection?

On the surface, the answer to this question appears obvious. After all, most people understand that *the main purpose of data collection is to determine student progress toward IEP goals and objectives.* Toward this end, a shortsighted interpretation of this purpose is to be concerned solely with whether or not the student has met his or her goals and objectives at the end of the year. While the determination of student progress at year's end is important, data collection is far more than the end result of a year's worth of work on a given objective—at least it ought to be. In fact, *we consider "data-collection-as-an-annual-event" to be woefully inadequate!* Rather, we feel strongly that *data needs to be collected on a regular basis throughout the year in order to help determine the following:*

- The student's rate of learning;

- The student's response to the methodology that is being employed;

- The student's response to prompts/cues and whether they are being faded back over time;

- Whether or not the goal or objective needs to be revised as a result of early achievement, slower than expected progress, or other factors; and,

- Whether or not there is adequate attention to the generalization of skills.

It should be obvious from the foregoing that the collection of data, *on a regular basis,* is a multifaceted activity, and one that is an essential part of the IEP process. In fact, the information amassed from the collection of data serves as the "fuel" that "drives" clinical decision-making. Moreover, data collection at regular intervals ensures that such decision-making is carried out in a timely manner, so that it may be used to make "mid-course" corrections in each of the areas noted in the bulleted list above, if deemed necessary. Conversely, if data collection occurs only on an annual basis, there will be little to no opportunity to make changes in practices that might be inimical to student progress or well-being.

It is also important to note that even when evaluation procedures are beyond reproach, the formulation of IEP goals and objectives still requires a good deal of conjecture/educated guesswork regarding the amount of progress that students can be expected to make in a given year. Despite the margin for error that this creates, mid-year IEP modification meetings are still relatively rare. There are two main reasons for this. First, educators and clinicians may be either unaware of the need to monitor student progress on a regular basis, or content to maintain the status quo rather than schedule yet another meeting. Second, those professionals who are cognizant of the need to consider mid-course adjustments in the IEP, often assume the responsibility of making those adjustments on their own, without input from the IEP team. Indeed, this is not only unacceptable from a "best practices" perspective, but also a violation of the intent of *IDEA* which champions *team* decision-making. Interestingly, when modification meetings do take place, they are typically at the request of parents who want to ensure that the goals and objectives for their children are continuously updated to meet their changing needs. The bottom line on this important subject is that, *while it is certainly important for parents to stay apprised of their children's progress, and to call for additional IEP meetings when needed, it is equally important for professionals to be similarly cognizant of their students' progress so that they, too, can initiate the process of IEP modification and adjustment.* Suffice it to say that anything short of this type of vigilance is, in our opinion, inimical to student success.

How Often Does One Really Need to Take Data?

There is no simple, universal answer to this question, as the timing of data collection is dependent upon a variety of factors. *In some cases, the collection of data may be methodology-driven.* For example, in most discrete trial or applied behavior analysis (ABA) training programs, data collection is ongoing (i.e., occurring at all times during the student's treatment sessions). In other treatment modalities, *data collection is guided by the student's rate of learning.* Thus, a more able student with a higher rate of learning would be expected to progress more quickly, creating the need for relatively frequent data collection. Similarly, a less able student with a slower rate of learning would likely require less frequent data collection. Below are some guidelines governing the frequency of data collection:

- *Methodology:* In general, the more structured the treatment session, the more frequently data collection may be expected to occur (e.g., discrete trial training). Conversely, when the setting is less structured (e.g., a community setting or other naturalistic context), data collection is generally less frequent.

- *Student's rate of learning:* As stated above, the faster the student makes progress, the more frequent data collection needs to be. A student who learns at a slower rate often requires less frequent data collection.

- *Demands of the learning situation:* In one-on-one situations, the demands on the instructor are often lower, allowing for more frequent data collection. More demanding situations (e.g., group lessons, community or naturalistic settings, etc.) require careful orchestration among teaching, monitoring, and data collection. In these situations, it is often more practical to take data at periodic intervals (e.g., weekly, bi-weekly) throughout the year.

- *Frequency with which the goal or objective is addressed:* When a goal or objective is addressed frequently (e.g., every day) it is reasonable to take data on a more periodic basis (e.g., weekly). Objectives that are addressed less frequently (e.g., once per week), as may be the case in a speech or occupational therapy session, however, may require that data be collected each time the objective is addressed.

- *Frequency with which the behavior is seen:* If a behavior is seen infrequently, it may be easy to keep a record of every instance in which the behavior occurs. If, on the other hand, the behavior occurs frequently, the team may wish to use a *time sampling procedure* whereby data is taken during a specific time interval (e.g., one hour per day; five minutes per hour, etc.).

- *Type of data being collected:* Simple quantitative data systems allow for easy and frequent collection. Qualitative systems, however, may require a narrative description or subjective rating of performance. These factors add complexity to data collection, and require more time and effort. As a result, practicality may dictate that data be compiled on a less frequent basis.

The foregoing guidelines illustrate that there is a data collection "spectrum," if you will, (from high-frequency collection schedules to low-frequency schedules) against which IEP objectives may be "evaluated" to determine the particular schedule that best fits the objective in question. Below are examples of some of the more common data collection schedules found in IEPs:

- Daily (throughout the day, each occurrence)
- Once per week
- Bi-weekly
- Once per month

The bottom line on data collection schedules is that they need to fit the contours of the behavior addressed in the objective, and they need to be specified within the IEP document. Many states contain specific sections on their IEP forms for this purpose. When this is not the case, such information needs to be included within the body of the objective, itself.

How Can One Ensure That the Data Collected Reflect Meaningful Student Progress?

The answer to this question is inextricably intertwined with the question of what should be measured. While this issue was addressed, in depth, in Chapter 5, some additional guidelines are offered here:

- First, the behavior to be measured must have either a *direct* or *indirect* impact on student functioning.

- Second, it must be clearly defined to ensure that all who address it respond in the same manner.

- Third, prompt levels, and the plan for fading them back, must be clearly specified, to ensure movement toward independent functioning.

- Finally, the measurement system selected should be capable of accurately measuring progress toward the goal (e.g., percentages are inappropriate for many behaviors).

Ideally, if the criteria are stated effectively, the means and schedules for data collection should follow naturally. It should be obvious from the foregoing that the effective measurement of student progress toward IEP objectives requires an in-depth understanding of the synchronous relationship that exists among the target behaviors selected, and the criteria, prompt levels, and data collection methods in service to them.

When Is *Quantitative* Measurement Appropriate?

The quantitative measurement of data is not only the easiest type to collect and analyze, but also the method of choice for most IEP teams. The main reason for the latter is that quantification inspires a certain comfort level among team members that other less precise data collection methods leave to be desired. For one thing, quantitative data offers definitive information; that is, one can determine at a glance whether or not the student has met the objective. Judgments about the *quality* of the behavior are not necessary since there is a clear distinction between "correct" and "incorrect." As a result, errors in analysis are often limited to errors in mathematical calculation.

Several means of quantitative measurement are available to IEP teams. Two of the most common methods are detailed below:

- *Tally System:* The easiest form of quantitative measurement to use, this system involves a simple tally of correct and incorrect responses. Following collection, the percentage of correct responses is calculated. This type of system is best used with criteria that measure performance in *percentage, specific number,* or *fraction* form.

- *Time Measurement:* When criteria specify a *specific amount of time* or a *time fraction,* time-based data may be gathered using a clock, stopwatch, finger count, or other method for recording information.

Quantitative data may also be obtained using specific evaluation procedures that yield numerical scores. For example, a speech-language pathologist may specify as a criterion level a specific mean length of utterance (MLU) (e.g., 2.5). This MLU may be calculated quantitatively through the analysis of a language sample.

Unfortunately, there is a downside to this preference for quantitative data collection. Simply stated, sometimes it is applied in situations that do not lend themselves to quantification. Consider the following example:

> *Given cues as needed, Heather will carry on a conversation with an adult or a peer—80%*

One might ask what the *80%* refers to: 80% of the time with an adult? 80% of the time with a peer? 80% of the conversation needs to be accurate? Or, 80% of the time she is required to engage in a conversation? The final question that should be asked is *and who's counting anyway?!* In other words, *quantitative data collection should not be used to assess behaviors that cannot be quantified. Likewise, neither should nonsensical "percentages" based upon the alleged "data" be reported as "evidence" of progress!*

When is *Qualitative* Measurement Appropriate?

Despite the appropriateness of quantitative measures for many of the types of behaviors typically addressed in IEPs, as noted above, *there are nonetheless some behaviors that simply cannot and should not be addressed by quantitative means.* While this topic was addressed briefly in Chapter 5, it deserves to be revisited here. Hence, at the risk of belaboring this very important point, *while IDEA clearly requires that goals and objectives be measurable, the law does not specify the means by which this should be accomplished.* It should be obvious that the choice of the particular method of data collection is left up to the IEP team, and further, that this choice should be based upon appropriateness and common sense. Lest the reader denigrate the use of qualitative measures as somehow inferior to those that are quantitative, we offer the following as "evidence" of the usefulness of qualitative data: Diagnosis of the syndrome of autism, itself, is made via *qualitative*, as opposed to quantitative judgments regarding an individual's behavior. Furthermore, when one compares more able students with ASD to their neurotypical peers, the most pronounced differences between the two are often seen in the subtle, *qualitative* ways in which those with ASD process information and express behavior. *Clearly, what is needed is an eclectic system of assessment that makes use of both quantitative and qualitative data, depending upon the particular type of skill-related or behavioral information desired.* In addition, many target behaviors are not served well by indicating that they are either present or absent. Rather they need to be judged for their qualitative *appropriateness* in a given situation or circumstance.

Because of the subjective nature of qualitative data, a word of caution is in order. Judgments regarding the appropriateness of behavior are in "the eye (or ear) of the beholder." In other words, there is often disagreement among members of the IEP team regarding the appropriateness of particular behaviors, since standards for acceptable performance will vary from person to person when there are no objective parameters by which to assess them. In addition, behaviors that involve very subtle judgments lead to even greater confusion.

One way of ensuring attention to these difficulties is to be mindful of them, on the theory that "to be forewarned, is to be forearmed." Another is for the IEP team to take a few moments within the meeting to define what it means by *appropriateness* vis-à-vis particular behaviors. In addition, the parameters for judging behavior should be revisited periodically to ensure that each team member continues to evaluate student performance in a similar manner.

Once the IEP team has clearly defined the behaviors that need to be measured, a system of data collection must be delineated. There are two primary means of analyzing qualitative aspects of behavior. These are described below along with examples for each type of data system.

- *Rating Scales:* A predetermined scale is created for the purpose of making qualitative judgments about a student's performance of a particular behavior. The scale should contain enough information to ensure that a given behavior is judged in a similar manner by different raters. Rating scales provide a practical means of *quantifying*, if you will, the *qualitative* process of judging the appropriateness of the student's behavior. Consider the following rating scale, designed for use with a student who uses an inappropriate volume when speaking:

    - Level 1: Student uses appropriate conversational volume (i.e., individuals in close proximity to the student are not disrupted)

    - Level 2: Student's vocal volume is moderately high (i.e., individuals within a 7-foot radius are disrupted, but others are not affected)

    - Level 3: Student's vocal volume is excessively high (i.e., individuals within a 15-foot radius are disrupted by the loudness of the student's voice)

A similar scale can be designed for a student whose speech volume is too soft, or whose rate of speech is inappropriate. In addition, rating scales can be used for many other behaviors that require qualitative judgments. When using rating scales, as when using quantitative measures, it is important to evaluate the target behavior(s) at regular intervals. The schedule for evaluation should be determined on the basis of both the factors described earlier, and the individual requirements of the particular school district.

- *Narrative Description:* This data collection method is often used to assess progress in such amorphous skill areas as social skills development and problem solving. Narrative description can also be used to supplement quantitative measures, such as tallies, particularly when judgments regarding the quality of performance are desired. Consider the following example:

> *Given prior review of problem solving strategies, Philip will solve problems, or seek the assistance of others that can help him, in the vocational setting, 4/5 opportunities, given expectant waiting.*

In the above example, narrative description can provide an effective way to monitor the manner in which the student applies problem solving strategies, as well as the timeliness and appropriateness with which he enlists (or fails to enlist) the help of others. Finally, since narrative descriptions require less precision, they are "user friendly" in the sense that they are relatively easy to generate.

Before leaving this topic, it is important to note that the use of narrative description is not without controversy, since it is the method of data collection most open to interpretation. In fact, the flexibility in data collection that narrative description affords creates an even greater need for a clear and detailed definition of behavioral expectations at the time the IEP is being developed or reviewed. Clear definitions will go a long way toward providing assurance that the narrator will observe, and therefore describe, the appropriate behavior.

Chapter 9

An IEP Potpourri: Other Considerations

In tackling a subject as multifaceted and complex as that of the individualized education plan, it is necessary to make decisions regarding those elements that require in-depth coverage, and those that can be well served with a broader, less detailed brush stroke. Our main focus in the preceding chapters has been on those elements of the IEP that have been the hardest hit by the "quality shortage" that plagues many present day IEPs. This is not to say that the elements covered in the preceding chapters are the only aspects of the IEP worthy of our attention, simply that they have the most direct impact on educational programming. In this chapter we cover those elements that, for our purposes, can be handled with a broader stroke. These include the *least restrictive environment (LRE)* provision of *IDEA; program modifications and supports for school personnel;* what is meant by the terms *modifications* and *accommodations;* and consideration of *related services* and *supplementary aids and services.*

LRE Requirement Under *IDEA*

(b) Each public agency shall ensure—

    (1) That to the maximum extent appropriate, children with disabilities, including children in public or private institutions or other care facilities, are educated with children who are non disabled; and

    (2) That special classes, separate schooling or other removal of children with disabilities from the regular educational environment occurs only if the nature or severity of the disability is such that education in regular classes with the use of supplementary aids and services cannot be achieved satisfactorily.

20 U.S.C. § 1412(a)(5)

A "Place" Called LRE

Ironically, while the IEP elements covered in the previous chapters were becoming mere shadows of their former "selves," the *LRE* provision of *IDEA* was developing greater clout with each passing year, at least from the point of view of interpretation of its intent. In other words, by the dawn of the new millennium *IDEA'S preference* for the least restrictive environment began to take on the properties of a "demand note." The *LRE's* front and center position within the IEP coincided with the inclusive education movement that began as a small snowball rolling down the hill in the mid 1980s, only to become a veritable avalanche toward the end of the 1990s. In fact, the commitment to *LRE* has become so strong that, as noted earlier in this book, many school districts across the United States have abandoned their special education classrooms in deference to the inclusive classroom setting. Freely translated, the *LRE* has become a *place* called the mainstream, rather than a *programmatic option* to be determined according to the needs of each individual student! It's time to set the record straight on this important issue.

It is indeed true that the requirement that children with disabilities be educated in the least restrictive environment is at the very core of *IDEA*. It is also true that *access* to the mainstream is an absolute right of students with disabilities. The question then is, does the *right* to be mainstreamed supercede the *right* to an *appropriate* education, if the mainstream environment is considered *inappropriate* for the student? We feel strongly that the answer to this question is a resounding *no*. In fact, we would argue that, in order to determine the appropriate classroom setting for a student with ASD—or for any other student for that matter—the following question needs to be asked: *Where does the student do his or her best learning?* If the answer to this question is the inclusive classroom setting, then that is where the student should be placed. If, however, the answer to the question is that the student learns best in a less complex, specialized environment, in which there are fewer students and less distractions, then a more restrictive setting would be in order. Needless to say, the answer to this question would probably vary vis-à-vis academic subject/activity. That said, in our opinion, *to honor a particular setting (i.e., the inclusive classroom) over the specific needs of the student is to glorify form over substance to the detriment of the child's educational success.*

We feel that we are on fairly secure legal (not to mention logical!) grounds with respect to the issue of *LRE*. We base this assertion upon the fact that despite *IDEA's preference* for inclusion, it nonetheless recognizes that for some students with disabilities, the inclusive classroom may not be the least restrictive environment in which they can derive educational benefit. To wit, in the citation of the law related to *LRE* above, it is clear that such language as "*to the maximum extent appropriate*" confers a *relative* standard on *LRE* decisions that ties the determination regarding placement to the particular needs of the student. In addition, according to Siegel (2001):

- First, LRE is really a characterization of a placement or program, not necessarily a specific place...

- Second, the LRE placement for a child is primarily the location of the program, but should also involve the programmatic components—for example, the size of the class, the kinds of children and the type of school (p. 2/5).

From the point of view of appropriateness and what is in the best educational interests of the student, we think that Attorney Siegel is right on!

Before leaving the topic of *LRE*, we'd like to turn briefly to the subject of what to do when there is no place other than the mainstream in which to place the student. In other words, what's a parent to do when the school's commitment to *LRE* causes it to offer no option but the inclusive classroom setting to a student who needs a specialized environment? *Clearly, from the perspective of what's in the best educational interests of the student, this is unacceptable.* It would also seem to be contrary to the *intent* of *IDEA,* which mandates that schools build programs around students according to their individual needs, rather than fit students into programs—mainstream or otherwise, and possibly inappropriate—simply because they're "the only game in town." Support for this position comes from Wright and Wright (1999/2000):

> In all cases, placement decisions must be individually determined on the basis of each child's abilities and needs, and not solely on factors such as category of disability, significance of disability, *availability of special education and related services, configuration of the service delivery system, availability of space, or administrative convenience"* [italics added] (p. 211).

Hopefully, Wright and Wright will have the final word on this very important subject. If not, perhaps this one will suffice—*Amen!*

Program Modifications and Supports

Requirement Under *IDEA*

(iii) ... a statement of the program modifications or supports for school personnel that will be provided for the child:

    (I)   to advance appropriately toward attaining the annual goals:

    (II)   to be involved and progress in the general curriculum in accordance with clause (i) and to participate in extracurricular and other non-academic activities; and

    (III) to be educated and participate with other children with disabilities and nondisabled children in the activities described in this paragraph; (1/11)

20 U.S.C. § 1414 (d)(1)(A)

The wording of the law noted above— "a statement of program modifications and supports *for school personnel that will be provided for the child*" [italics added]—directly links the supports for school personnel to outcomes for students. In essence, this provision of *IDEA* does "double duty," in that it focuses on the needs of both school personnel and students.

The Florida State Department of Education (2000) defines supports for school personnel as, "services provided directly to the regular teacher, special education teacher, or other school personnel to assist a student with disabilities to be involved or progress in the general curriculum" (p. 80). While *services* can refer to a variety of things, one of the first things that come to mind is that of in-service education. Indeed, it may be said that *IDEA* sets forth a mandate for adequate knowledge and training on the part of school personnel who serve students with disabilities. Consider the language used in Part B of the law whereby it sanctions the use of "paraprofessionals and assistants *who are appropriately trained and supervised,...* [italics added] to... assist in the provision of special education and related services to children with disabilities..." (as cited in Wright & Wright, 1999/2000, p.47). In fact, *IDEA* directs the local education agency (LEA) to "ensure" that school personnel are "appropriately and adequately prepared" to deliver educational services to students with special needs (as cited in Wright & Wright, 1999/2000, p. 53). The Florida State Department of Education (2000) notes that supports for school personnel may include "specific training or specific staff development activities to ensure that school personnel have the knowledge, information, skills, and materials needed to help the student" (pp. 80–81). It lists additional supports as follows:

• "consultant services,

• collaborative teaching, or

• assistance from a paraprofessional or teacher aide" (p. 81).

Clearly, IDEA recognizes the importance of adequately trained staff, and holds LEAs accountable for ensuring that school personnel have the knowledge and skills necessary to deal appropriately with students with disabilities. As noted in many sections of this book, nowhere does the importance of an adequate knowledge base loom larger than in the case of autism, given its enigmatic nature and many challenges. Furthermore, according to Wright and Wright (1999/2000), "Program modifications and *supports* for school personnel can be written into the child's IEP" (p. 62).

The Little Known, But Important Distinction Between *Accommodations* and *Modifications*

In addition to its position regarding support for school personnel in the form of training and in-service education, *IDEA* also advocates *direct* support for students with disabilities in the form of modifications and accommodations. Even Section 504 of the Rehabilitation Act— *under which students eligible for services under IDEA receive automatic protections*—clearly requires that "reasonable accommodations" be made for students who require them (Wright & Wright, 1999/2000, p. 262). Although the terms are more often than not used interchangeably, there are important differences between *modifications* and *accommodations* that have significant implications for students with disabilities.

As the term *accommodation* implies, the emphasis is on *obliging* the student so that he or she is more available for learning, if you will. This can be done by removing, to the extent possible, barriers to success, or by increasing the circumstances favorable to successful performance. Accommodations may be made to the following:

- Instructional methods, teaching style and delivery, and curricular materials
- Classroom and homework assignments
- Assessment tools and practices
- Time requirements
- The environmental setting
- The manner and type of student output (e.g., oral recitation / computer for fine motor difficulty)

According to Twachtman-Cullen (2001, February 23)

> Accommodations refer to the adjustments that are made to ensure that the students with disabilities have both equal access to educational programming, and the means by which to demonstrate success. Once accommodations

are made, *students with special needs are expected to meet the standards for all students* [italics added] (p. 10).

It should be obvious from the foregoing, that *accommodations are not intended to create a different (i.e., lower) standard for students with ASD, but rather to enable the student to meet the expectations specified for all students.* Basically, accommodations are intended to empower school personnel to do what it takes to "get around" the limitations imposed by the student's disability. As such, accommodations are important accoutrements for the inclusive classroom setting, since they can spell the difference between success and failure for the student with ASD. Before turning our attention to modifications, it is important to underscore the following important points:

- Accommodations are not limited to those areas listed above, but rather are confined only by the boundaries of one's creativity and imagination.

- It is not only the *responsibility*, but also the *obligation* of the school to accommodate the student with ASD.

- Accommodations should be thoroughly discussed by the IEP team and *documented* within the body of the IEP.

To summarize, when schools fail to provide students with the accommodations they need to meet with educational success, they, in effect, (albeit by default) *require* students with disabilities to accommodate to programming that is not individualized to their needs, and which may be inimical to their interests. That this would be an inadvertent by-product of the lack of accommodations does not change the fact that it would be a violation of both the intent and spirit of the law. Finally, documentation of the accommodations within the IEP ensures that all who provide instruction to the student will be using the same procedures.

It should be obvious that the term *modification* implies *change*. Hence, it is fundamentally different from the term *accommodation*. According to Twachtman-Cullen (2001, February 23), "Modifications... refer to substantive changes in course/subject delivery, content or instructional level that have the effect of creating a different standard for students with disabilities" (p. 10). While there is some degree of overlap between the terms *accommodations* and *modifications,* there is one crucial difference between them—that of *educational outcomes.* In other words, unlike accommodations, *modifications can create a different (i.e., lower) standard for students with ASD, such that they would not be expected to meet the curricular requirements and educational standards of the mainstream environment.*

Modifications may be made to the educational program itself. Hence, students with ASD may receive a very different curriculum from that of their neurotypical peers. There may also be modifications within all of the areas listed above for accommodations, the major difference being that the standards for performance would be *adjusted* (i.e., lowered or changed) in some significant manner. Having said that, a word of caution is in order. The tendency to use the terms *accommodations* and *modifications* interchangeably can have a profound and deleterious impact upon service delivery, particularly if team members are unaware of the implications that these terms have for standards of performance. For one thing, it can cause parents to *assume* that their children are meeting grade-level expectations in cases where this is clearly not the case. Hence, given the potential for unintended, but nonetheless misleading information regarding standards of performance, it is vitally important that the IEP team not only discusses and clearly delineates what it intends with respect to accommodations and modifications, but also that it acknowledges the important distinction between the two concepts. Moreover, it is also important that accommodations and modifications be documented within the IEP, so that everyone is "on the same page" with respect to understanding. Finally, it is crucial to note that while paraprofessional support staff can and should assist the professional staff in providing accommodations for students, when needed, these staff members should not assume responsibility for *decision making* with respect to modifications. That task is strictly within the purview of certified staff. Furthermore, if paraprofessional support staff are assigned the job of implementing teacher/clinician generated modifications, they should do so only under the supervision of certified personnel.

Assessment Considerations

In a related area, for those students for whom formal assessment is considered appropriate, *IDEA* calls for "a statement of any individual modifications in the administration of State or district-wide assessments of student achievement that are needed in order for the child to participate in such assessment" (Siegel, 2001, Appendix 1/11). It should be obvious that the distinction between *accommodations* and *modifications* would loom large here, as well. In other words, accommodations would consist of those adjustments that would enable the student with ASD to *meet the assessment expectations set for all students.* Modifications, on the other hand, would create a *different* standard for performance. In fact, if accommodations alone are unsuccessful in enabling students to participate in State or district-wide testing, *IDEA* requires that the IEP team document *how* the child will be assessed. Indeed, if the extent of the testing modifications required by the student is so great as to create a materially different test and assessment standard, then alternate assessment techniques must be provided. Many states and school districts list the accommodations that they sanction in their assessment protocols. Where these are not adequately stated, a good rule of thumb to follow is that the types of accommodations for testing should be similar to those used successfully in the instructional program.

Finally, if educators are careful to delineate the differences between accommodations and modifications, and to discuss the implications of each of these on student performance, they will go a long way toward helping parents to view their children's educational progress and status more realistically. As such, parents would be less likely to misinterpret the grades their children receive. For example, a grade of *A* on a science test where only accommodations have been used, is vastly different from a grade of *A* on a test in the same subject where modifications have significantly lowered the standards for acceptable performance. Unfortunately, it has been our experience that the important distinction between accommodations and modifications is not always made clear to parents.

Related Services and Supplementary Aids and Services

Requirement Under *IDEA*

(iii) a statement of the special education and related services and supplementary aids and services to be provided to the child, or on behalf of the child...

    (I)   to advance appropriately toward attaining the annual goals;

    (II) to be involved and progress in the general curriculum in accordance with clause (i) and to participate in extracurricular and other non-academic activities; and

    (III) to be educated and participate with other children with disabilities and nondisabled children in the activities described in this paragraph;

(iv) an explanation of the extent, if any, to which the child will not participate with nondisabled children in the regular class and in the activities described in clause (iii);

20 U.S.C. § 1414 (d) (1)(A)

The intent of the law seems quite clear. The IEP team must provide documentation within the IEP of the following:

- The special education services required;

- The related services, and supplementary aids and services required; and

- The extent, if any, to which the student will not participate in the regular education program.

The logical time to make these decisions is after the IEP team has discussed the student's present levels of performance (PLP), drafted annual goals and short-term objectives or benchmarks, and considered the need for program accommodations, modifications, and supports. It will be remembered that the requirement under the PLP provision of *IDEA* is that the team must also consider the impact of the child's disability vis-á-vis his/her involvement in the general curriculum, or for preschool children, in appropriate activities.

The Distinction Between Support Categories

There is a good deal of confusion between what is meant by *related services* versus *supplementary aids and services*. IDEA defines *related services* as, "transportation and such developmental, corrective, and other supportive services as are required to assist a child with a disability to benefit from special education…, (as cited in Siegel, 2001, Appendix 1/21)" According to Siegel (2001) counseling and therapeutic services are included within this category. He also includes the following:

- "Sign language or oral interpreter…

102

- One-to-one instructional aide...

- Art therapy [and]

- Technological devices, such as FM/AM systems or special computer..." (Siegel, 2001, p. 2/6).

Siegel is careful to note that his list is not "exhaustive," since determinations regarding related services are made on an individual need basis.

IDEA defines *supplementary aids and services* as, "aids, services, and other supports that are provided in regular education classes or other education-related settings to enable children with disabilities to be educated with nondisabled children to the maximum extent appropriate..." (as cited in Siegel, 2001, Appendix 1/23). While *education-related settings* are open to interpretation, the term undoubtedly has the effect of broadening the scope of this provision beyond the walls of the regular education classroom.

Wright and Wright (1999/2000) distinguish between the terms as follows:

- *Related services* are services that the child needs to benefit from special education....(p. 29).

- *Supplementary aids and services...* means, **aids, services,** and **other supports** that are provided in **regular classes** or **other education-related settings** to enable children with disabilities to be educated with nondisabled children to the maximum extent appropriate (p. 30).

We believe that the distinction stated above provides the best explanation of the differences between these two related concepts, particularly with respect to how the *related services* provision relates to special education, and how the *supplementary aids and services* provision addresses regular education. According to the Florida State Department of Education (2000), supplementary aids needed by students with disabilities may include:

• adapted materials and

• specialized equipment used in regular classes,

• such as large-print textbooks,

• recorded materials, or

• specially designed software.

Supplementary services may include

• note takers,

• sign language interpreters and

• personal assistants (p. 108).

It should be obvious that there is overlap between the two categories. To wit, Siegel (2001), above, includes sign language interpreters and personal assistants under the category of *related services,* while the Florida State Department of Education (2000) includes the two under the category of *supplementary aids and services.* Which interpretation is correct? The answer is that *both* are correct. Specifically, students with disabilities, regardless of whether they are served in inclusive or special education settings, often need the same, or similar supports. Hence, the same service may be appropriate to either category—*related services* or *supplementary aids and services*—depending upon the particular educational setting. Clearly, the benefit to the student with ASD is that all bases are covered!

Part Two:

IEP Goal and Objective Templates

Chapter 10

Assessment and Decision Making in the Designing of Effective IEPs

Having discussed the essential elements of the IEP in terms of the *intent* of *IDEA* in Part 1 of the book, it is now time to translate the law's intent into practical application. Since this is often easier said than done, as the many examples of poor practice interspersed throughout this book illustrate, in this chapter we attempt to provide the reader with guidelines for bridging the gap between "theory" (i.e., the law) and practice (i.e., writing IEPs based upon the letter and spirit of the law). We also offer the reader a "guided tour" through the remaining chapters of the book.

In order to write IEPs that deliver appropriate educational programming for students with ASD, we believe the following "prerequisites" are necessary:

- Adequate, research-based knowledge of the many facets of ASD

- Assessment information regarding the unique strengths, weaknesses, and needs of each individual student with ASD across several, specific areas of functioning

- The means for determining *priority* educational needs

- A comprehensive understanding of the essential elements of the IEP

Research-Based Knowledge of ASD

In recent years, research into the characteristics and needs of individuals with ASD has resulted in an ever-expanding knowledge base. Where in the not-so-distant past autism was defined predominantly in terms of its effect upon *social behavior, communication/language, restricted interests/ impoverished imagination,* and *abnormal response to sensation,* today we know that other areas of cognitive and social-cognitive functioning are also at-issue. Specifically, in addition to the problems seen in the areas specified above, students with ASD also manifest difficulty in *executive function, theory of mind, information processing,* and *critical thinking.* Hence, IEPs can no longer address only the "traditional" areas of deficit delineated previously, but must also consider those cognitive and social-cognitive areas of functioning that research and clinical practice have revealed to be problematic.

Toward this end, we have put together an at-a-glance guide to a) make it easier for IEP teams to consider some of these additional areas and, b) provide a "road map" to direct the reader through the remaining chapters of the book. The *Goal & Objective Selection Matrix* presented in Table 2 contains broad-based goal categories for *Comprehension; Communication, Expression, and Oral-Motor Skills; Social Interaction, Play, and Leisure Skills;* and *Cognitive and*

Social-Cognitive Skills. We have included the category of *oral-motor skills* since, according to Rogers and Bennetto (2000), oral-motor dyspraxia is a major contributor to lack of speech development in some students. The broad-based goal categories are listed along the left margin of the table, while the more specific content areas that flow from these categories are contained within the body of the table. (See following two pages for Table 2.)

Table 2

GOAL & OBJECTIVE SELECTION MATRIX

LESS ABLE	MORE ABLE
Comprehension • Concept Development ■ Core ■ Concrete • Verbal Language • Vocabulary Development • *Following Directions* • *Wh Questions*	• Concept Development ■ Abstract • Verbal Language ■ Figurative Speech ■ Multiple Meanings of Words • Story Narratives • Vocabulary Development ■ Attributes/Description ■ *Following Directions* ■ *Wh Questions* • Nonverbal Cues & Signals
Communication, Expression, & Oral-Motor Skills • Pragmatics (Basic Functions) ■ Behavioral Regulation (Requesting, Protesting) ■ Social Interaction (Obtaining Attention) ■ Joint Attention (*Sharing Attention/* Commenting) • Oral-Motor Skills ■ Oral Sensitivity ■ Oral-Motor Planning ■ Sound/Speech Production	• Pragmatics (Higher Order Functions) ■ Using Repair Strategies ■ Asking Questions ■ Negotiating ■ *Directing* ■ *Answering Questions* • Conversational Rules • Presuppositional Knowledge • Story Building/Narrative Discourse • Sentence Formulation • Word Retrieval

110

	LESS ABLE	MORE ABLE
Social Interaction, Play, & Leisure Skills	• Social Interaction ■ Responding/Social Reciprocity ■ Basic Turn-taking ■ *Social Engagement* • Play Skills Development ■ *Parallel Play* ■ *Associative Play* • Leisure Skill Development	• Play Skills Development ■ Using Social Scripts ■ Interactive Play • Following Social Rules/ "Sizing Up" Social Situations • Social Interactive Games • *"Small Talk"*
Cognitive & Social-Cognitive Skills	• Executive Function ■ Using Scheduling Systems/ Transitioning ■ Basic Planning • Critical Thinking ■ Prediction ■ Problem Solving	• Executive Function ■ Planning/Time Management ■ Self-Monitoring ■ Impulse Control • Critical Thinking ■ Prediction ■ Making Inferences ■ Problem Solving ■ *Determining Relevance* ■ *Drawing Conclusions* • Theory of Mind/ *Perspective Taking*

Objectives for the italicized areas in the Table above may be found under the category of *Miscellaneous Short-term Objective Templates* at the end of each of the chapters.

It is from these goal categories and content areas that we fashioned the sample goals and objectives amplified in the remaining chapters of this book. Specifically, rather than addressing academic goals and objectives related to *math, science, history*, and the like, we confine ourselves to writing goals and objectives for those areas specified in the *Matrix*. We do so for two main reasons: 1) because these areas of functioning are typically impacted in ASD; and, 2) because deficits in these domains are often sorely neglected in students' IEPs. There are many reasons for the latter, not the least of which include lack of recognition that problems exist, or lack of knowledge regarding what to do about them when they are detected.

In no way do we intend this *Matrix* to contain an exhaustive listing of *all* of the problem areas affected in ASD, but rather, those areas that we feel require further illumination, based upon the reasons stated above. It should be noted that, while we break down the broad-based goal categories into subheadings related to functioning level (i.e., less able/ more able), we do so only as a convenience to the reader. In fact, we fully acknowledge that for some students the distinction between ability levels is often arbitrary, largely subjective, and not always clear-cut. This is particularly true for very young students. Hence, there can be a good deal of overlap across functioning levels, particularly in young children.

Finally, in order to emphasize the critical importance of using research-based knowledge of ASD as the supportive framework for generating meaningful IEP goals and objectives, we include a research-based rationale for each of the goal areas addressed in chapters 11 through 14. We include this information not only to underscore the important role that research plays in the generation of goals and objectives, but also to provide a model for IEP teams to follow as they plan educational programs for students.

Assessment Considerations

While a broad-based general knowledge of ASD is the lynch-pin around which appropriate programming revolves, it alone will not suffice in meeting the standard of *individual-ization* set forth in *IDEA*. In other words, in order to satisfy the goal of providing an educational program that is *indi-vidualized* to the specific needs of particular students, one must understand how the symptoms of ASD play out in each particular student. Hence, assessment of the student's strengths and weaknesses is integral to the generation of IEP goals and objectives that are individualized to his/her needs. In fact, documentation of strengths and weaknesses forms the basis of the present levels of performance (PLP) state-ment that serves as the standard by which priority needs are derived, and progress is judged.

While an in-depth discussion of various types of assessment tools is well beyond the scope of this book, a few points on this important topic are nonetheless in order. First and fore-most, the reader is cautioned against becoming an "assess-ment snob;" that is, one who views *formal* evaluation as innately superior to *informal* assessment. Indeed, decisions regarding whether to use formal or informal assessment tools should not be viewed from an *either-or* perspective. In our opinion, *both types of assessment are important*, since they gen-erate different types of information under vastly different conditions and circumstances. As such, when appropriately applied, they complement, rather than detract from one another. Furthermore, formal test results alone may be mis-leading for students at both ends of the autism spectrum. For example, many of the formal tests for assessing the pragmatic communication and language needs of more able students lack the sensitivity to unmask their subtle language compre-hension and use difficulties. When this occurs, their compre-hension and language use issues go unnoticed, and hence, untreated. In addition, formal tests are not yet available for many of the cognitive and social-cognitive deficits associated with ASD. Moreover, formal assessment may not be possible, at all, for students at the less able end of the autism spectrum, or for those with significant behavioral challenges.

All things considered, as a general rule of thumb, we advocate the use of informal assessment procedures across a variety of contexts and activities for *all* students with ASD, regardless of functioning level. We also recommend the use of formal assessment tools for those students for whom this type of testing is *reasonable* and *defensible*; however, we do so with the caveat that scores and percentile ranks be viewed with extreme caution, and that such testing be supplemented by informal procedures. Finally, we advocate that educators and clinicians not only view assessment as a dynamic and ongoing process, rather than a "one-shot" event, but also that they be mindful of the ways in which autistic symptomatology can interfere with assessment and cloud test results.

The Determination of Priority Educational Needs

While in some cases it may be possible to design goals and objectives for all of the deficit areas requiring attention in ASD, in most cases, this is not possible, due to the number of problem areas that typically require remediation. Since the IEP is intended to address the *annual* goals and objectives that the school hopes to accomplish during a given year, an important part of IEP decision-making requires that teams prioritize those areas of functioning that need immediate redress, versus those that can be put on temporary hold. In some cases, the process of establishing priorities is relatively easy. This is particularly true when dealing with behaviors that pose a danger to the student or to his or her classmates, since such behaviors, by their very nature, demand immediate attention. Most of the time, however, determining the student's priority educational needs can be more of an art form than a scientific endeavor.

114

The following general guidelines are offered to help IEP teams determine the priority educational needs that will serve as the foundation for the annual goals and objectives for students:

- Be logical! *Select early developing behaviors and skills first.*

- Be sensible! *Select behaviors and skills that the student has a reasonable chance of learning.*

- Be wise! *Select behaviors and skills that will make a significant and meaningful difference in the student's life.*

To operate according to these guidelines doesn't require "rocket science," as the saying goes. What it does require, however—and what may be in shorter supply than rocket science—is common sense, an appreciation for developmental considerations, and sensitivity to the role of functionality and relevance in the lives of students with ASD. The form entitled, *Priority Educational Need Analysis,* located at the end of this chapter, is offered to provide the reader with a systematic approach for establishing priority educational needs for these students. This user-friendly rating scale takes into account the following parameters:

- Severity

- Frequency

- Functionality/Relevance

- Developmental Readiness

- Importance to the Family

A Comprehensive Understanding of the Essential Elements of the IEP

At this point, it should be eminently clear to the reader that we consider the essential elements of the IEP to be crucial to *appropriate* education and *effective* service delivery. To wit, we granted each element its own chapter in Part 1 of the book, in order to provide in-depth coverage regarding the pivotal role that each of these elements plays in IEP development. We now offer the reader The *IEP Essential Elements Checklist*. This form—also located at the end of this chapter—is intended to fulfill two important functions:

- First, to serve as a reminder for IEP teams to attend to all of the important elements of the IEP, even those that they might, otherwise, be tempted to leave to chance.

- Second, to help promote accountability in IEP development, overall.

Overview of Remaining Chapters

The following four chapters represent our attempt to "translate theory into practice." Hence, we take the information presented in Part 1 of the book and *apply* it to the actual practice of writing annual goals and short-term objectives for students with ASD. Our aim in these chapters is twofold:

- First, to illustrate how the essential elements of the IEP may be melded together to generate coherent goals and objectives for students with ASD; and,

- Second, to give the reader specific direction in applying the information presented in Part 1 to the writing of goals and objectives for the content areas delineated in the *Goal & Objective Selection Matrix*.

As was the practice in the case of the essential elements of the IEP, each one of the next four chapters is devoted to a single, specific area of functioning. Each of these corresponds to the goal categories listed in the *Matrix*. These are as follows: *Comprehension; Communication, Expression, and Oral-Motor Skills; Social Interaction, Play, and Leisure Skills;* and *Cognitive and Social-Cognitive Skills.*

Each chapter in Part 2 is formatted in the same manner, and contains the following components:

- A brief, research-based rationale to help the reader understand why students with ASD typically require remediation in the particular areas of functioning covered within the chapter
- A list delineating the specific type of information required in the PLP for the above-noted areas
- The particular content areas covered within the chapter
- Sample PLPs
- Templates for annual goals and short-term objectives

It is important for the reader to keep in mind that the goals and objectives presented in these chapters are offered as *templates*, rather than as finished products. In fact, the reader should construe them as the "builder's models," discussed in the construction metaphor in the *Introduction* of this book. As such, they are, by design, "incomplete." In other words, while we parenthetically refer to *criteria, prompt levels/fade back plan, generalization protocol,* and *evaluation procedure and schedule,* we do not provide specific examples of these elements, except in cases where they might be difficult to ascertain. We leave these areas open for three reasons:

1. To allow IEP teams maximal flexibility in using these templates for their own purposes

2. To provide a framework within which IEP teams may individualize these elements to suit the needs of the particular student and situation

3. To provide IEP teams with a greater impetus for consulting the individual chapters that address each of these essential elements

In fact, at the risk of redundancy, *we strongly urge the reader to consult the chapters in Part 1 of the book that correspond to the essential elements of the IEP listed parenthetically within the short-term objective templates.*

117

It should be noted that, in keeping with the generic nature of these templates, we use the impersonal designation *Student*, in place of an actual name. Further, while we do not intend Part 2 of the book to serve as an "objectives bank," per se, we nonetheless encourage IEP teams to use the templates for students with similar needs, provided that they *individualize* them with respect to content and circumstance.

Given our commitment to practical application, we have included three additional sections within each of the next four chapters. The first is *Recommended Educational Programming Formats*. These consist of 17 instructional contexts represented by the letters *A* through *Q*. In our opinion, each one of these contexts provides an excellent milieu for working on IEP goals and objectives. Since these formats are universally applicable to the goal and objective templates in chapters 11 through 14, we elected to place the *complete* list of recommended formats in *Appendix A*, to avoid redundancy. We do, however, list the formats by letter alone, for each of the goals specified in the chapters. Finally, it should be specifically noted that the *Recommended Educational Programming Formats* are intended for use in both *skill development* and *generalization* activities. Hence, their inclusion within the chapters reflects both uses.

The second section referred to above is entitled *General Teaching Tips & Strategies*. These consist of a potpourri of ideas, delivered in "stream of consciousness" fashion, that we have found particularly useful when addressing the skill areas covered within the chapters. Since these lists have been individualized with respect to chapter content, they may be found at the end of chapters 11 through 14.

Third, we present a list of *Useful Teaching Resources* for each of the content areas addressed in Part 2. It comprises the final section of each chapter, and contains resources, in abbreviated form, specific to those areas of functioning covered by the goal and objective templates in each of the chapters. The more expanded list of resources may be found in *Appendix B.* This list is by no means exhaustive. In fact, there are several other excellent resources that we were unable to include, given the constraints of this project. Hence, the reader is urged to seek out additional teaching resources on his/her own.

To summarize, the information and forms contained within this chapter are intended to streamline the decision making process, and enable IEP teams to more systematically address the prerequisites to generating meaningful IEP objectives based upon the individual needs of students with ASD. We now turn our attention to applying what we know to the heart of the IEP process.

PRIORITY EDUCATIONAL NEED ANALYSIS

Student's Name: _____ DOB: _____

Subject Area/Domain: _____ IEP dated from: _____ to _____

Proposed Goal/Objective:_____

_____

_____

_____

Rate the proposed goal/objective along the parameters specified by circling the number that best applies. When finished, add the numbers and divide by 5 to determine the *Educational Need Composite Score*. Compare this score to those for other proposed goals/objectives for the purpose of determining whether or not there exists a priority educational need. This worksheet is not designed to replace sound clinical judgment. Rather, it is designed to help facilitate need prioritization.

A. Severity

Mild difficulty   1   2   3   4   5   Severe difficulty

B. Frequency

Infrequently required skill/behavior   1   2   3   4   5   Frequently required skill/behavior

C. Functionality/Relevance

Non-functional/ Non-relevant   1   2   3   4   5   Functional/ Relevant

D. Developmental Readiness

Late developing skill/ Prerequisites not yet mastered   1   2   3   4   5   Early developing skill/ Prerequisites mastered

E. Importance to Family

Unimportant   1   2   3   4   5   Very important

Results:

Sum of Ratings: _____ /5 = Educational Need Composite Score: _____

Priority Need Analysis (e.g., low, moderate, high): _____

IEP Essential Elements Checklist

☐ Are the *present levels of performance* statements sufficiently informative to serve as the basis for generating annual goals and objectives, as well as the standards by which to judge progress?

☐ Are the *underlying conditions* clearly delineated for each objective?

☐ Are *methodology* and *context* specified, and/or taken into account in the designing of short-term objectives?

☐ Are the *criteria* for objectives meaningful, appropriate, and sufficient to permit judgment of performance?

☐ Are *prompt levels* specified, and is there ongoing attention to the systematic fading back of prompts over time?

☐ Is there evidence of attention to *generalization* and *maintenance* of skills across activities, settings, and people?

☐ Do the long-term *annual goals* follow from the present levels of performance, and are they well-stated and reasonable for the period specified?

☐ Do the *short-term objectives* follow logically from the goals, and are they meaningful, clearly stated, and measurable?

☐ Are *evaluation/data collection* procedures meaningful, and are they employed at regular intervals?

☐ Is sufficient consideration given to *LRE* requirements?

☐ If *accommodations, modifications,* and/or other *supports* are necessary, are they specifically documented in the IEP?

☐ Are all *related services* and *supplementary aids and services* clearly specified in the IEP?

☐ Does the IEP reflect the student's *priority educational needs* for the coming year?

Chapter 11

Sample IEP Goal and Objective
Templates for Comprehension

Rationale for Inclusion of This Skill Category:

- Comprehension generally *precedes* production in both typical children and those with developmental disabilities (Sevcik & Romski, 1997).

- Research demonstrates that concept development is an area of difficulty in students with ASD (Goldstein, Minshew, & Siegel, 1994; Minshew, Goldstein, Taylor, & Siegel, 1994).

- The pragmatic deficits seen in students with ASD do not just occur in the expressive areas of pragmatics. Deficits are also found in *receptive* areas. (Twachtman-Cullen, 2000c).

- Difficulty with language comprehension has been documented in even the most able students with ASD. Students at this end of the autism spectrum tend to interpret language very literally, and have difficulty understanding figurative language and speaker intent (Peeters & Gillberg, 1999).

- In addition to difficulty with language comprehension, students with ASD also have difficulty comprehending nonverbal cues and signals (Landa, 2000; Mundy & Sigman, 1989; Tantum, 2000).

Present Levels of Performance for Comprehension Skills Should Include:

- A statement indicating the student's strengths in comprehension skills, particularly as they relate to overall functioning.

- A statement regarding the student's weaknesses in specific areas of comprehension, particularly as they relate to priority educational needs for the coming year.

- A statement of how the student's disability in comprehension impacts his/her involvement and progress in the general curriculum (or for preschool children, in appropriate activities)

- The source(s) of the statement(s) in the PLP.

- Any additional information that can enable the PLP to fulfill its two important functions: 1) *to serve as the basis for generating need-based, individualized IEP objectives*; and, 2) *to serve as the standard by which to judge performance/ progress.*

CONTENT AREA:
Concept Development—Core and Concrete

Sample PLP for a 7-year-old student with severe autism and mental retardation: *Student presents with receptive language skills that would be most consistent with those of an 18-month-old child, based upon observational data and parent report. While he demonstrates comprehension of several core concepts, on the basis of their function (i.e., he knows how to use a whistle, cup, sock, and shoe), he does not yet know them as object labels (i.e., he is not able to identify them when asked). Student's severe difficulty with language comprehension and concept development impacts his ability to understand much of what goes on in the school environment, and impedes his ability to participate effectively in school activities in both his special education classroom and the mainstream settings to which he is assigned.*

Goal/ Objective Templates Based Upon PLP:

Annual Goal: Student will demonstrate comprehension of concepts as specified in, and measured by short-term objective(s).

Short-term Objective: Given direct teaching and multi-sensory experiences, Student will demonstrate comprehension of (specify number) functional core and concrete concepts by responding appropriately to them in contextually relevant activities, (specify criteria) given (specify prompt levels/fade back plan and generalization protocol e.g., across a minimum of [specify number] different settings, activities, and people). (Specify evaluation procedure and schedule.)

Recommended Educational Programming Formats: A, B, C, D, E, F, K, L, M, O, Q

CONTENT AREA:
Concept Development — Abstract

Sample PLP for a 4-year-old student with high-functioning autism (HFA): *Student demonstrates understanding of many core and concrete concepts that serve her well in her preschool classroom. She has a great deal of difficulty with abstract, relational concepts (e.g., prepositions). For example, she insists that someone is in TV, rather than on TV, since from her perspective the person is "inside" the television. Student's parents state that she can become quite insistent, to the point of having tantrums. Her teacher reports that the other children are beginning to react negatively to her when this type of behavior occurs in the classroom. Student's confusion over prepositions also makes it difficult for her to follow directions in many of the activities in her preschool environment.*

Goal/Objective Templates Based Upon PLP:

Annual Goal: Student will demonstrate comprehension of developmentally appropriate abstract concepts as specified in, and measured by short-term objective(s).

Short-term Objective: Given direct instruction and accompanying manual signs, Student will demonstrate comprehension of (specify number) prepositions by responding appropriately to directives involving them in contextually appropriate activities and situations, (specify criteria) given (specify prompt levels/fade back plan and generalization protocol). (Specify evaluation procedure and schedule.)

Recommended Educational Programming Formats: A, B, C, D, E, F, K, L, M, O, Q

126

CONTENT AREA:
Verbal Language

Sample PLP for a 5-year-old student with severe autism and mental retardation: *According to teacher and parent report, Student's comprehension skills have improved greatly this year. Currently, informal and formal assessment indicates that his receptive language skills cluster in the 18–24 month range. While he has demonstrated comprehension of several one-step directions when presented in context, (e.g., "sit down," "come here," and "stand up"), he is not always consistent in doing so. These difficulties impact both his ability to follow directions, and to understand the verbal language needed to participate fully in his preschool program.*

Goal/Objective Templates Based Upon PLP:

Annual Goal: Student will demonstrate improvement in the comprehension of verbal language as specified in, and measured by short-term objective(s).

Short-term Objective: Given direct instruction, and the use of manual signs to accompany verbal directives, Student will demonstrate comprehension of (specify number) new functional one-step directions in contextually relevant activities, (specify criteria) given (specify prompt levels/fade back plan and generalization protocol). (Specify evaluation procedure and schedule.)

Explanatory notes:

- Accompanying manual signs aid the processing of verbal information. As such, it is important to bear in mind that there are times when it is *inappropriate* to fade them back. This is particularly true in cases where there is a severe auditory or information processing problem, and/or when the number of directives given makes it difficult for the student to process the information on an auditory basis alone.

- If, on the other hand, there are circumstances in which the student *demonstrates* the ability to comprehend specific verbal input without accompanying manual signs, then these cues may be faded back.

- All things considered, *the decision to fade or not to fade back manual signs is a judgment call that should be based upon student need/performance.*

Recommended Educational Programming Formats: A, B, C, D, E, F, J, K, L, M, O, Q

Sample PLP for a 15-year-old student with HFA: *Student's comprehension skills serve her well in one-on-one and small group situations (e.g., the resource room/therapy room), according to both her teacher and speech-language pathologist. She has difficulty comprehending verbal language as sentence length and complexity increase, particularly in more complex environments (e.g., inclusive classroom settings). She also has difficulty when asked to give a verbal response to a question "on the spot." These difficulties negatively impact both her participation in inclusive classroom activities and her grades, overall.*

Goal/Objective Templates Based Upon PLP:

Annual Goal: Student will demonstrate improvement in the comprehension of verbal language as specified in, and measured by short-term objectives.

Short-term Objective 1: Given the *pre-teaching* of subject areas earmarked for group discussion in academic classes, and practice opportunities, Student will demonstrate comprehension of verbal language by answering questions appropriately in role-play situations in the resource room, (specify criteria) given (specify prompt levels/fade back plan and generalization protocol). (Specify evaluation procedure and schedule.)

Short-term Objective 2: Given the *pre-teaching* of subject areas earmarked for group discussion in academic classes, and practice opportunities, Student will demonstrate comprehension of verbal language by generating written notes in answer to specific questions about the material in the resource room, (specify criteria) given (specify prompt levels/fade back plan and generalization protocol). (Specify evaluation procedure and schedule.)

Short-term Objective 3: Given the *pre-teaching* of subject areas earmarked for group discussion, prior practice, and student-generated notes on the material, Student will demonstrate comprehension of verbal language by answering questions about the material within the inclusive academic settings for (specify subjects), (specify criteria) given (specify prompt levels/fade back plan). (Specify evaluation procedure and schedule.)

Explanatory note: The last objective in the set above represents the final step in a 3-step process designed to move from a restrictive to an inclusive setting. As such, it requires no additional generalization protocol.

Recommended Educational Programming Formats: G, H, I, K, L, N

CONTENT AREA:
Verbal Language—Figurative Speech

Sample PLP for a 12-year-old student with pervasive developmental disorder—not otherwise specified (PDD-NOS): *Student's comprehension of language is quite good at the literal level, particularly when answering factual questions, according to his teacher, and as documented in formal testing. He has a great deal of difficulty with idiomatic expressions and figurative language, in general, both of which interfere with his overall comprehension. His teacher reports that lately, Student has become the target of ridicule by some of his classmates because of his literalness and lack of appreciation for jokes. These problems set Student apart from his classmates in his inclusive classroom settings.*

Goal/Objective Templates Based Upon PLP:

Annual Goal: Student will demonstrate comprehension of figurative language as specified in, and measured by short-term objective(s).

Short-term Objective: Given direct instruction in the meaning of selected figures of speech, Student will demonstrate comprehension of (specify number) idiomatic expressions embedded in context by responding appropriately to them in structured role-plays, (specify criteria) given (specify prompt levels/fade back plan and generalization protocol). (Specify evaluation procedure and schedule.)

Recommended Educational Programming Formats: A, G, K, L, M, N, O, Q

CONTENT AREA:
Verbal Language—Multiple Meanings of Words

Sample PLP for a 10-year-old student with HFA:
Student manifests strengths in spelling, and in using vocabulary in a straightforward, literal manner. Comprehension is adequate as long as words are used in the way that Student has learned them. He has significant difficulty, however, understanding words when they are used in ways that are unexpected. For example, when asked to define what was meant by the phrase, "a cold stare," Student replied, "It was cold in the room." According to his speech-language pathologist, Student has trouble understanding that words can have multiple meanings. Consequently, he is quite rigid in his adherence to the definitions that he knows. This problem impacts his ability to understand much of what goes on around him, and makes it difficult for him to process information in a timely fashion in his 5th grade inclusive classroom setting.

Goal/Objective Templates Based Upon PLP:

Annual Goal: Student will demonstrate improvement in understanding multiple meanings of words as specified in, and measured by short-term objectives.

Short-term Objective 1: Given prior direct instruction, a set of cards containing words that have multiple meanings (e.g., *train, play, cold,* etc.), and scenarios depicting (specify number e.g., 2, 3, etc.) different uses for each of the words presented, Student will verbally supply the word that matches each of the multiple-meaning scenarios, (specify criteria) given (specify prompt levels/fade back plan and generalization protocol). (Specify evaluation procedure and schedule).

Short-term Objective 2: Given prior direct instruction and (specify number) words that have 3–4 meanings each, Student will give at least (specify number e.g., 2, 3) meanings

131

of each word presented, (specify criteria) given (specify prompt levels/fade back plan and generalization protocol). (Specify evaluation procedure and schedule).

Short-term Objective 3: Given prior direct instruction, Student will demonstrate comprehension of multiple meanings of (specify number) words, by responding appropriately to them in structured role-plays, (specify criteria) given (specify prompt levels/fade back plan and generalization protocol). (Specify evaluation procedure and schedule).

Recommended Educational Programming Formats: A, C, F, G, H, K, L, M, N, O, Q

CONTENT AREA:
Story Narratives

Sample PLP for a 9-year-old student with Asperger syndrome (AS): *Student's strengths in narrative comprehension lie in her ability to remember the details of stories, many of which are irrelevant to the story line. According to her teacher, she has significant difficulty identifying character, setting, and problem. Student's narrative comprehension difficulty impacts her ability to perform adequately in all areas of the curriculum that involve an understanding of narrative information (e.g., reading, language arts, social studies, etc.).*

Annual Goal: Student will demonstrate comprehension of story elements as specified in, and measured by short-term objectives.

Short-term Objective 1: Given direct instruction in the use of a color-coded story board, Student will demonstrate an understanding of main *character(s), setting,* and *problem* by selecting pictures appropriate to the story line from a group of (specify number) options, for use in telling about targeted story elements across (specify number) different stories, (specify criteria) given (specify prompt levels/fade back plan and generalization protocol). (Specify evaluation procedure and schedule.)

Explanatory notes:
- This type of color-coded teaching tool can be provided as a follow-up to narrative assignments.
- Criteria should be specified for each story element (e.g., 8/10 opportunities for character; 8/10 opportunities for setting; 8/10 opportunities for problem).
- Different criteria may be specified for each story element, as well, particularly if the student demonstrates uneven performance in a given area(s).

Short-term Objective 2: Given cued opportunities, Student will demonstrate comprehension of stories as they are being read by an adult, by selecting story forms (e.g., objects, felt board characters, or pictures) depicting *character(s)*, *setting*, and *problem* across (specify number) different stories, (specify criteria) given (specify prompt levels/fade back plan and generalization protocol). (Specify evaluation procedure and schedule.)

Short-term Objective 3: Given cued opportunities, Student will demonstrate comprehension of story narratives by answering questions about *character(s)*, *setting*, and *problem* across (specify number) different stories, (specify criteria) given (specify prompt levels/fade back plan and generalization protocol). (Specify evaluation procedure and schedule.)

Recommended Educational Programming Formats: E, F, G, K, L, M

CONTENT AREA:
Vocabulary Development

Sample PLP for a 7-year-old student with moderate autism: *Reportedly, Student is minimally verbal (i.e., at the 1–2 word response level), but has made a lot of progress this year in the area of comprehension. His understanding of vocabulary, however, is distributed inconsistently across themes, according to his speech-language pathologist and teacher. In addition, his rate of vocabulary learning is barely at the 1–word level per theme unit. While student is beginning to understand some of the more experientially based concepts such as the verbs "go," "stop," "push," "pull," and the concepts "big" and "little," his grasp of them is sketchy, at best. These difficulties impact his ability to follow directions in a timely fashion, and to derive benefit from the curriculum in both the resource room and his inclusive classroom setting.*

Goal/Objective Templates Based Upon PLP:

Annual Goal: Student will demonstrate comprehension of vocabulary words as specified in, and measured by short-term objective(s).

Short-term Objective: Given multi-sensory experiences within a functional theme-based curriculum, Student will demonstrate comprehension of (specify number) vocabulary words per thematic unit by answering simple questions and/or engaging in appropriate actions involving them, (specify criteria) given (specify prompt levels/fade back plan and generalization protocol). (Specify evaluation procedure and schedule.)

Recommended Educational Programming Formats: A, B, C, D, E, F, L, O, Q

CONTENT AREA:
Vocabulary Development—
Attributes/Description

Sample PLP for a 16-year-old student with AS: *Despite the fact that Student has a large and relatively sophisticated vocabulary, she has difficulty comprehending directives in both her day-to-day school activities and in her social skills group. Her speech-language pathologist reports that in observing student during her participation in a game involving clues, it is apparent that she does not comprehend many of the attributes, as judged by her erroneous responses to the questions of her peer buddy. Student's comprehension difficulty impacts her ability to understand verbal directives, and to process information in a timely fashion in her 10th grade inclusive classroom settings.*

Goal/Objective Templates Based Upon PLP:

Annual Goal: Student will demonstrate comprehension of attributes/descriptors as specified in, and measured by short-term objective(s).

Short-term Objective: Given direct teaching and accompanying visual cues, Student will demonstrate comprehension of (specify number) attributes/descriptors by responding appropriately to contextually relevant questions in activities designed for this purpose, (specify criteria) given (specify prompt levels/fade back plan and generalization protocol). (Specify evaluation procedure and schedule.)

Recommended Educational Programming Formats: C, K, L, M, O, Q

CONTENT AREA:
Nonverbal Cues and Signals

Sample PLP for a 13-year-old student with HFA: *Both informal observation within academic settings, and testing via the Peabody Picture Vocabulary Test—Revised (PPVT—R) indicate that Student has adequate vocabulary development for his age. This serves him relatively well in class discussions, as long as distractions and noise are kept to a minimum. Unfortunately, his prowess in verbal comprehension contrasts sharply with his ability to comprehend the nonverbal cues and signals that accompany verbal input, particularly as they relate to sarcasm and irony. His teachers report that Student is often the object of ridicule and teasing because he takes what he hears literally, and fails to take into account the tone of voice or body language that change the meaning of the words. This problem leaves Student at-risk for being "set up" by his peers.*

Goal/Objective Templates Based Upon PLP:

Annual Goal: Student will demonstrate improvement in the comprehension of nonverbal cues and signals as specified in, and measured by short-term objectives.

Short-term Objective 1: Given *direct* teaching and sample observational vignettes, Student will demonstrate the ability to discriminate between literal and sarcastic utterances by selecting the correct characterizations of each within a forced-choice format, (specify criteria) given (specify prompt levels/fade back plan and generalization protocol). (Specify evaluation procedure and schedule.)

Short-term Objective 2: Given *indirect* cues and sample observational vignettes, Student will demonstrate the ability to discriminate between literal and sarcastic utterances by selecting correct responses to them within a multiple choice format, (specify criteria) given (specify prompt levels/fade back plan and generalization protocol). (Specify evaluation procedure and schedule.)

Short-term Objective 3: Given scaffolding in the form of increased time and structured role-plays, Student will demonstrate the ability to discriminate between literal and sarcastic utterances by responding to them appropriately, (specify criteria) given (specify prompt levels/fade back plan and generalization protocol). (Specify evaluation procedure and schedule.)

Recommended Educational Programming Formats: A, C, G, K, L, M, N, O, Q

Miscellaneous Short-term Objective Templates for Comprehension Development

The generic objective templates that follow address additional areas of comprehension that are often found to be problematic in ASD. They are offered not only to provide the reader with additional examples of comprehension objectives, but also to stimulate thinking regarding the ways in which teachers, clinicians, and parents can work together to shore up this crucial, foundational area. We invite the reader to use the objectives presented, if applicable, and to individualize them to suit the particular student and situation. In so doing, *we urge readers to keep uppermost in their minds that effective service delivery requires that annual goals and instructional objectives follow logically from well-stated PLPs.*

Short-term Objective 1: Given direct teaching and accompanying manual signs, Student will demonstrate comprehension of (specify number) verbal utterances/directives by responding appropriately to them in contextually relevant situations and activities, (specify criteria) given (specify prompt levels/fade back plan and generalization protocol). (Specify evaluation procedure and schedule.)

Short-term Objective 2: Given prior direct teaching and accompanying manual signs (i.e., for *where, who*), Student will demonstrate comprehension of (specify number) *where* and *who* questions, by responding appropriately to them in contextually relevant situations and activities, (specify criteria) given (specify prompt levels/fade back plan and generalization protocol). (Specify evaluation procedure and schedule.)

Short-term Objective 3: Given attention to, and interest in the activity, Student will follow simple 1-step directions given by an adult or a peer within a game-like format (e.g. *Simon Says*), (specify criteria) given (specify prompt levels/fade back plan and generalization protocol). (Specify evaluation procedure and schedule.)

Short-term Objective 4: Given a daily schedule and *indirect* cues, Student will demonstrate the ability to follow classroom routines/activities with minimal adult assistance by engaging in the appropriate action/behavior, (specify criteria) given (specify prompt levels/fade back plan and generalization protocol). (Specify evaluation procedure and schedule.) (Example of indirect cue: *"What is it time to do?"* vs. *"Go check your schedule."*)

Short-term Objective 5: Given an array of (specify number) small, stationary objects (e.g., "doll house" table, chair, stove, etc.), Student will demonstrate comprehension of prepositions by placing (specify number) other moveable objects (e.g., apple, shoe, pan) in various places vis-à-vis the stationary items (e.g., *in, on, under, next to,* etc.) within a barrier game activity with a peer, (specify criteria) given (specify prompt levels/fade back plan and generalization protocol). (Specify evaluation procedure and schedule.)

Explanatory note: Barrier game activities, also known as *referential communication tasks*, are ideal vehicles for the development of language *comprehension* and *expression*. Speech-language pathologists typically have a good deal of information on many different types of barrier games, as well as knowledge of the various ways in which they can be used to shore up language development, overall.

General Teaching Tips & Strategies for Comprehension

1. Provide students with frequent, repetitive language input, delivered in short units of speech, and with accompanying manual signs/visual supports, whenever possible.

2. Avoid *testing* students by constantly asking questions. Instead, *teach* them by providing the information they need to establish the connections that lead to meaning.

3. Organize the curriculum around concepts and vocabulary that are functional for the student (i.e., that directly relate to the student's life experiences).

4. In working with themes or curriculum units, select those that are conceptually-based and/or functionally relevant (e.g., for younger students: sticky/smooth theme; big/little theme, etc.; for older students: going to a restaurant; doing the laundry, etc.). Moreover, be sure to organize these in such a manner that the student is able to understand the unifying elements that comprise the theme/unit.

5. Conduct experiential, multi-sensory, hands-on lessons to facilitate comprehension of word-object, word-action, and object-action associations, and to promote comprehension beyond the level of the simple object label.

6. Make use of multiple-choice formats, where appropriate, particularly in the initial stages of skill development, as they help to structure the student's responses, thereby enabling him/her to be more successful.

7. Utilize techniques and strategies that facilitate the student's ability to process information and understand directives. These include:

141

- Securing the student's attention *before* giving a direction
- Simplifying language processing by breaking down multi-step directions
- Adding visual information to the directions:
  - Objects and/or object miniatures
  - Picture cues
  - Natural gestures
  - Sign language (i.e., manual signs)
- Reducing extraneous auditory and visual distractions to the extent possible
- Encouraging the student to use repair strategies (e.g., to ask for repetition/clarification), when needed

8. Directly teach the meaning of idiomatic expressions and figurative language in a context that underscores their meaning.

9. Directly teach students to understand the meaning of nonverbal cues and signals in both contrived and natural situations. Provide practice opportunities, *in context*, through the use of structured role-plays.

10. Utilize color-coding and visual supports to concretize and directly teach difficult-to-grasp narrative elements.

Useful Teaching Resources

(See *Appendix B* for additional information.)

1. *Concept Acquisition Procedures for Preschoolers (CAPP): Levels 1, 2, & 3.* By C. Weiner.

2. *Conceptbuilding: Developing Meaning Through Narratives and Discussion.* By P. Reichardt.

3. *Early Communication Skills.* By C. Lynch & J. Kidd.

4. *Excell: Experiences in Context for Early Language Learning.* By C.B. Raack.

5. *Figurative Language: A Comprehensive Program.* By K. A. Gorman-Gard.

6. *Helping the Child Who Doesn't Fit In.* By S. Nowicki, Jr. & M. P. Duke.

7. *Interactive Language Skills.* By J.G. DeGaetano.

8. *Listen My Children And You Shall Hear.* By B. Kratvoville.

9. *Listening, Understanding, Remembering, Verbalizing!* By J.G. DeGaetano.

10. *Narrative Tool Box: Blueprints for Story Building.* By P. Hudson-Nechkash.

11. *Telling a Story.* By M. M. Toomey.

12. *Themestorming.* By J. Becker, K. Reid, P. Steinhaus, & P. Wieck.

13. *This is the One That I Want.* By L.G. Richman.

14. *Understanding the Nature of Autism: A Practical Guide.* By J. Janzen.

15. *Visual Strategies for Improving Communication.* By L. Hodgdon.

Chapter 12

Sample IEP Goal and Objective Templates for Communication, Expression, and Oral-Motor Skills

Rationale for Inclusion of This Skill Category:

- Pragmatics is the primary area of communication difficulty in students with ASD (Twachtman-Cullen, 2000a, 2000b, 1998).

- Wetherby and Prutting (1984) state that the pragmatic functions of communication develop according to the following order in students with ASD :

    - The *behavioral regulation* functions develop first (e.g., requesting, protesting).

- The *social interaction* functions develop second (e.g., obtaining attention, turn-taking).

- The *joint attention* functions develop third (e.g., commenting).

- Some students at the less able end of the autism spectrum may not develop joint attention functions (Curcio, 1978; Sigman, Mundy, Sherman, & Ungerer, 1986).

• More able students with ASD may also have difficulty with the use of higher-order pragmatic functions (Gillberg & Ehlers, 1998; Twachtman-Cullen, 2000a, 2000b, 1998) such as:

- Use of repair strategies

- Negotiating

- Dealing with sarcasm/irony, etc.

• Difficulties are also seen in two additional areas of pragmatics (Twachtman-Cullen, 2000a, 2000b, 2000c):

- Presuppositional knowledge (This involves the ability to adjust one's speech to the needs of the listener and situation.)

- Conversation/Discourse (This involves the ability to adhere to the rules governing conversational interaction (e.g., *quantity, quality, relevance,* and *clarity,* Grice, 1975.)

• Narrative discourse skills are often negatively impacted in students with ASD, as a result of the documented deficits in critical thinking (Minshew, Goldstein, Taylor, & Siegel, 1994; Twachtman-Cullen, 2000b, 2000c).

• Clinical experience reveals that many less able students with ASD are either nonverbal or minimally verbal.

• Individuals with ASD present with deficits in "complex motor abilities or praxis" (Minshew, 1996). These difficulties often result in impaired oral-motor and/or speech

146

production skills (Rogers & Bennetto, 2000). A recent study found *direct* evidence of oral-motor and motor-speech difficulty in individuals with ASD (Adams, 1998).

- The sensory processing and modulation difficulties seen in students with ASD, and related disabilities, often extend to the mouth in the form of oral sensitivity issues (Mackie, 1996).

- Because sensation drives movement, oral-sensory issues can directly impact the individual's ability to produce speech (Boshart, 1998). Areas of oral sensitivity include:

  - Tactile (i.e., touch/texture) Difficulty here can impact the student's ability to feel where his/her tongue, lips, and other articulators are.

  - Proprioceptive (i.e., sensation in oral muscles and jaw joints) Difficulty here can impact the student's ability to sense the amount of force needed to chew foods, or to know how to position his/her tongue, lips, etc.

  - Gustatory (i.e. taste)

- Although oral-motor difficulties may affect students with ASD at all ages and functioning levels, these problems are most prominent in students at the less able end of the autism spectrum. Moreover, according to Rogers and Bennetto (2000), "one reason for the lack of speech development in some children with autism is an underlying oral-motor dyspraxia" (p. 95). *Dyspraxia*—also referred to as *apraxia*—stems from motor planning difficulty.

Present Levels of Performance for Communication, Expression, and Oral-Motor Skills Should Include:

• A statement indicating the student's strengths in specific areas of communication/expression, or oral-motor skills. If addressing pragmatic functions, indicate the specific pragmatic functions for which the student is able to communicate.

• If the student is nonverbal or minimally verbal, it is helpful to include the student's current means of communication.

• A statement regarding the student's weaknesses in specific areas of communication/expression, or oral-motor skills, particularly as they relate to *priority* educational needs for the coming year.

• A statement of how the student's disability in communication/expression, or oral-motor functioning impacts his/her involvement and progress in the general curriculum (or, for preschool children, in appropriate activities).

• The source(s) of the statement(s) in the PLP.

• Any additional information that can enable the PLP to fulfill its two important functions: 1) *To serve as the basis for generating need-based, individualized IEP objectives;* and, 2) *To serve as the standard by which to judge performance/progress.*

CONTENT AREA:
Pragmatics—Behavioral Regulation:
Requesting/Protesting

Sample PLP for a 5-year-old student with severe autism:
*The Student's teacher and speech-language pathologist report
that she is quite self-sufficient; that is, when she wants something, she will try to obtain it on her own. For example, if
something is on a high shelf, student will typically bring a chair
over to the area, and attempt to climb on it to obtain what she
desires. If a chair is unavailable, she will sometimes lead the
adult to the object of choice. While Student is able to give a photograph in an exchange format to request something, given
cues, she does not appear to look at the photograph, nor connect
it to the item she receives. Student's primitive, nonverbal communication skills often cause her a good deal of frustration. In
addition, they not only prevent her from participating effectively in her special education classroom, but also limit her
mainstream experiences.*

Goal/Objective Templates Based upon PLP:

Annual Goal: Student will demonstrate improvement in the
pragmatic communication skill of requesting as specified in,
and measured by short-term objectives.

Short-term Objective 1: Given the desire to eat and drink,
and the presence of *preferred* food and beverage items,
Student will request items desired by (specify means e.g.,
handing representational object to the adult), (specify criteria) given (specify prompt levels/fade back plan and
generalization protocol). (Specify evaluation procedure and
schedule.)

Explanatory notes:

- This objective lends itself to the following prompt fade
  back plan: adult asking *"What do you want?"* with hand

extended to receive small object cue; proceeding to a *direct* verbal (e.g., *"What do you want?"*), then to an *indirect* verbal cue (*"I have cheese and crackers."*), and then proceeding to gestural cue alone, expectant waiting, and finally to independent/initiated.

- To insure that *requesting* is fully functional for the student, the generalization protocol should include participation in this activity across different food and beverage choices, across different people (e.g., speech-language pathologist, teacher, paraprofessionals, etc.), and across different settings (e.g., classroom, therapy room, cafeteria).

- Since the above-stated PLP clearly indicates that the child was not attending to the pictures, this objective specified a more concrete requesting mode in the form of objects.

- Additional objectives can be written for pictures when the child is ready for this step.

Short-term Objective 2: Given the desire to eat and drink, and the presence of *preferred* food and beverage items, Student will *initiate* requests for items when presented with a snack tray by (specify means e.g., handing a representational object or picture to the adult), (specify criteria), (specify generalization protocol e.g., across settings; communication partners; a variety of food/beverage items). (Specify evaluation procedure and schedule.)

Explanatory notes:

- Prompt levels do not need to be specified since the student is required to *initiate* requests in this objective.

- Additional objectives should be written to expand requesting to other referents (e.g., toys, requests for a break, etc.)

Recommended Educational Programming Formats: A, C, D, J, K, L, M, O, Q

**Sample PLP for a 4-year-old student with moderate
autism:** *According to teacher and parent report, although
Student is minimally verbal, he is beginning to indicate his needs
by taking an adult to a particular object and shifting his gaze
from it to the adult. His teacher also reports that he is less frus-
trated than he was earlier in the year, owing to an improvement
in his ability to make his needs known. Student is able to use a
variety of appropriate means to protest (i.e., push-away gesture,
placing object into an "all done" box, saying "all done," using an
"all done" sign), as long as he is prompted to do so. Despite this,
most of the time, he protests or requests termination of activities
through the use of aberrant means such as throwing objects, or
dropping to the floor. His behavior affects his ability to engage in
preschool classroom activities without extensive supervision by staff.*

Goal/Objective Templates Based upon PLP:

Annual Goal: Student will demonstrate improvement in the
pragmatic communication skill of protesting as specified in,
and measured by short-term objectives.

Short-term Objective 1: When offered *non-preferred* items,
Student will reject undesired objects/activities by (specify
means, e.g., word—*No*; manual sign—*No*; push-away gesture;
placing object in an "all done" box, etc.), (specify criteria)
given (specify prompt levels/fade back plan and generalization protocol). (Specify evaluation procedure and schedule.)

Short-term Objective 2: Given (specify underlying condition, e.g., the presence of an "all done" box, picture cue,
etc.) Student will request termination of an activity by (specify means e.g., word—*Stop*; manual sign—*Finished*; placing
object in *"all done"* box, etc.), (specify criteria) given (specify prompt levels/fade back plan and generalization
protocol). (Specify evaluation procedure and schedule.)

Recommended Educational Programming Formats:
A, C, D, J, K, L, M, O, Q

CONTENT AREA:
Pragmatics — Social Interaction:
Obtaining Attention

Sample PLP for a 14-year-old student with moderate autism and mental retardation: *According to clinical observation and teacher report, Student is able to effectively communicate her desires during a classroom snack routine when staff is attending to her, or when they specifically ask her what she wants. When staff is not attending to her, however, she will just sit and wait for a prompt. Both her speech-language pathologist and teacher are concerned that she is becoming increasingly prompt dependent. These difficulties impact Student's ability to independently get her needs met in both her special education classroom and in the mainstream settings to which she is assigned.*

Goal/Objective Templates Based upon PLP:

Annual Goal: Student will demonstrate improvement in the pragmatic communication skill of obtaining attention, as specified in, and measured by short-term objectives.

Short-term Objective 1: Given direct teaching and demonstration/modeling, Student will obtain the attention of an adult prior to making a request by (specify means, e.g., calling name, tapping adult's arm, etc.), (specify criteria) given (specify prompt levels/fade back plan and generalization protocol). (Specify evaluation procedure and schedule.)

Short-term Objective 2: Given the use of *indirect* cues (e.g., *"I have cookies,"* or arm placed close to student), Student will obtain the attention of the adult prior to making a request, by (specify means, e.g., calling name or tapping adult's arm), (specify criteria) given (specify prompt levels/fade back plan and generalization protocol). (Specify evaluation procedure and schedule.)

Explanatory notes:

- Since the student is being asked to obtain the adult's attention, it is imperative that she not already have his/her attention!

- A third party "coach" should be used to prompt attention to the target adult, so that the student can *legitimately* obtain his/her attention.

Recommended Educational Programming Formats:
A, C, J, L, O, P, Q

CONTENT AREA:
Pragmatics—Joint Attention: Commenting

Sample PLP for an 11-year-old student with pervasive developmental disorder (PDD): *Student is able to verbally comment on present events as they are happening, according to teacher and parent report. She does not yet comment on past events, however, even when directly asked about them by her teacher or parents. These difficulties affect her ability to provide necessary information across school environments, and interfere with her ability to answer questions related to academic subjects.*

Goal/Objective Templates Based upon PLP:

Annual Goal: Student will demonstrate improvement in the pragmatic communication skill of commenting as specified in, and measured by short-term objective(s).

Short-term Objective: Given visual supports (e.g., a topic notebook from a field trip), and carrier phrases (e.g., *"Remember the funny...," "Look, he's..."*), Student will comment on a past activity/event to a novel person (i.e., one who did not participate in event originally) by (specify means, e.g., pointing to items in pictures, saying words, etc.), (specify criteria, e.g., 4/5 events/activities; may also specify frequency, e.g., number of times per day or per week task is performed), given (specify prompt levels/fade back plan e.g., adult questioning and cues; adult pointing only; expectant waiting, etc.). (Specify generalization protocol and evaluation procedure and schedule.)

Recommended Educational Programming Formats: A, B, J, K, L, M, O, Q

CONTENT AREA:
Pragmatics—Using Repair Strategies,
Asking Questions, and Negotiating

Sample PLP for a 12-year-old student with AS: *Student's
speech-language pathologist reports that he communicates for a
variety of purposes including obtaining attention, requesting,
protesting, and commenting. In fact, he appears to have
mastered most of the lower-level pragmatic functions of communication. He experiences difficulty, however, with higher-
order functions such as the use of repair strategies, asking
questions, and negotiating. These difficulties impact Student's
ability to function in his 7th grade inclusive setting, and in
extra-curricular activities, as well.*

Goal/Objective Templates Based upon PLP:

Annual Goal: Student will demonstrate improvement in the
use of language for communication purposes as specified in,
and measured by short-term objectives.

Short-term Objective 1: Given direct instruction and a variety of situations in which verbal clarification is needed,
Student will use appropriate repair strategies to inform the
listener of the need for additional information, (repair strategies to include: requests for clarification; requests for
repetition; statements indicating a lack of understanding),
(specify criteria) given (specify prompt levels/fade back plan
and generalization protocol). (Specify evaluation procedure
and schedule.)

Short-term Objective 2: Given accompanying manual sign
cues, Student will ask questions using *wh* and other question
forms in order to obtain *needed* information in contextually
appropriate situations and activities, (specify criteria) given
(specify prompt levels/fade back plan and generalization
protocol). (Specify evaluation procedure and schedule.)

Short-term Objective 3: Given direct instruction in negotiation techniques, and (specify number) structured "flexible" scenarios that lend themselves to further modifications, Student will select the appropriate negotiation strategy (specify strategies e.g., *"Please"; "Just a little longer"; "Can I do just one?"* etc.) from a group of (specify number) options presented, (specify criteria) given (specify prompt levels/fade back plan and generalization protocol). (Specify evaluation procedure and schedule.)

Short-term Objective 4: Given direct instruction, and (specify number) structured "flexible" scenarios that lend themselves to further modifications, Student will apply the appropriate negotiation strategy in structured role-play situations with a peer, (specify criteria) given (specify prompt levels/fade back plan and generalization protocol). (Specify evaluation procedure and schedule.)

Recommended Educational Programming Formats: A, B, C, H, I, K, L, M, N, O, Q

CONTENT AREA:
Conversational Rules

Sample PLP for a 14-year-old student with PDD: *By
teacher and parent report, Student appears to enjoy interacting with others. She will frequently approach adults and peers
to greet them. After the greeting, however, she appears unsure of
how to keep the conversation going. This difficulty impacts her
ability to interact socially with adults and peers in both curricular and extra curricular activities across inclusive settings.*

Goal/Objective Templates Based upon PLP:

Annual Goal: Student will demonstrate improvement in
conversing with adults and peers as specified in, and measured by short-term objectives.

Short-term Objective 1: Given direct instruction, demonstration, and modeling, Student will choose appropriate
"conversation fillers" from (specify number) options presented, to fill her turn in conversations with at least 1 adult/
peer in structured role-play situations, (specify criteria e.g.,
for a minimum of 3, 4, etc. turns; a gradually increasing
number of turns, etc.) given (specify prompt levels/fade
back plan and generalization protocol). (Specify evaluation
procedure and schedule.)

Short-term Objective 2: Given manual sign and picture
cues, Student will fill her turn in conversations with at least
1 adult/peer in structured role-play situations, (specify criteria) given (specify prompt levels/fade back plan and
generalization protocol). (Specify evaluation procedure and
schedule.)

Recommended Educational Programming Formats:
A, B, C, K, L, M, N, O, Q

Sample PLP for a 9-year-old student with AS: *Student is a very verbal child who enjoys discussing topics of interest with others, according to clinical observation and teacher report; however, Student has problems carrying on conversations with others when he does not choose the topic. Under these conditions, he has great difficulty staying on topic, as evidenced by his tendency to change the subject (usually to one that centers around his interests), and/or make tangential comments. This difficulty impacts his ability to communicate with both adults and peers, and is especially off-putting to the latter. Overall, Student's disability in this area of sociocommunicative functioning negatively affects his ability to establish relationships with peers in his inclusive classroom setting.*

Goal / Objective Templates Based upon PLP:

Annual Goal: Student will demonstrate improvement in topic maintenance as specified in, and measured by short-term objectives.

Short-term Objective 1: Given direct instruction in what it means to stay on topic, and discussion topics, not of his choosing, but containing elements that he finds *moderately* interesting, Student will demonstrate the ability to select conversational sentence strips from a group of (specify number) options presented that are appropriate to the topics, across (specify number) topics and (specify number) turns, (specify criteria e.g., 8/10 opportunities to select) given (specify prompt levels/fade back plan and generalization protocol). (Specify evaluation procedure and schedule.)

Short–term Objective 2: Given prior practice, manual sign cues, and discussion topics that he finds *minimally* interesting, Student will demonstrate the ability to stay on topic by filling his conversational turn with statements/questions that are appropriate to the topic under discussion, across (specify

number) topics and (specify number) turns in structured
role-plays with adults and peers, (specify criteria) given (specify prompt levels/fade back plan and generalization
protocol). (Specify evaluation procedure and schedule.)

Recommended Educational Programming Formats:
A, B, C, K, L, M, N, O, Q

CONTENT AREA:
Presuppositional Knowledge

Sample PLP for an 18-year-old student with AS:
According to formal testing, teacher observation, and parent report, Student has an excellent command of vocabulary, grammar, and syntax. She is doing very well in her academic setting where adults and peers who know her well, accept her social idiosyncrasies. Problems arise, however, in her school-related work-study program. Reportedly, she has made inappropriate, personal comments to both her supervisor and customers. Student's lack of appreciation for the situational requirements of the work setting place her at-risk for losing her job.

Goal/Objective Templates Based upon PLP:

Annual Goal: Student will demonstrate improvement in the element(s) of presuppositional knowledge as specified in, and measured by short-term objectives.

Short-term Objective 1: Given direct instruction regarding "business" vs. "personal" talk, demonstration/modeling of appropriate and inappropriate comments, and contrived work-related scenarios, Student will select from a multiple choice format statements or questions appropriate to a business setting, (specify criteria) given (specify prompt levels/fade back plan and generalization protocol). (Specify evaluation procedure and schedule.)

Short-term Objective 2: Given review of "business" vs. "personal" talk and contrived work-related scenarios, Student will apply the appropriate statement or comment that she selected in structured role-plays with an adult, (specify criteria) given (specify prompt levels/fade back plan and generalization protocol). (Specify evaluation procedure and schedule.)

Recommended Educational Programming Formats:
A, B, C, K, L, M, N, O, P, Q

CONTENT AREA:
Story Building / Narrative Discourse

Sample PLP for an 11-year-old student with HFA: *While Student presents with strengths in verbal skills, his narrative skills cluster at the 4- to 5-year-old level, according to informal assessment tasks. His narratives are characterized by disorganized heaps of information rather than a sequentially organized series of events. These difficulties strongly impact Student's ability to generate written narratives across academic subjects in his inclusive classroom setting, and generally interfere with his ability to demonstrate what he knows on quizzes and tests.*

Goal/ Objective Templates Based upon PLP:

Annual Goal: Student will demonstrate improvement in narrative discourse as specified in, and measured by short-term objective(s).

Short-term Objective: Given a color-coded story format with accompanying pictures, and instruction in its use, Student will generate a complete, written narrative containing the elements of *character, setting, time, event,* and *solution* across (specify number) different stories, (specify criteria) given (specify prompt levels/fade back plan and generalization protocol). (Specify evaluation procedure and schedule.)

Recommended Educational Programming Formats: E, F, G, H, K, L, M

Sample PLP for a 9-year-old student with AS: *Student presents with excellent decoding skills that place her well above her peers in this skill. When assessed using a multiple-choice format, she even appears to be able to comprehend "straight forward" (e.g., factual) information reasonably well. Problems occur, however, when she is asked to retell a story, or a past event. Under these circumstances, Student is "all over the board;" that is, she mentions things out of sequence, or she fails to mention them at all. This difficulty impacts Student's ability to participate in language arts and reading activities in her fourth grade inclusive classroom, as well as in other activities involving narrative discourse.*

Annual Goal: Student will demonstrate improvement in reformulating narratives from events and stories as specified in, and measured by short-term objectives.

Short-term Objective 1: Given direct instruction in using a time line template for sequencing, and visual supports corresponding to a recent past event (e.g., photographs of a field trip or other event), Student will place the pictures in the appropriate sequence as she retells the event, incorporating the following elements: *participants, setting, time*, and at least one *activity,* across (specify number) events, (specify criteria) given (specify prompt levels/fade back plan and generalization protocol). (Specify evaluation procedure and schedule.)

Short-term Objective 2: Given visual supports corresponding to a recent past event (e.g., photographs of a field trip or other event), Student will retell the event, incorporating the following elements: *participants, setting, time*, and at least one *activity,* across (specify number) events, (specify criteria) given (specify prompt levels/fade back plan and generalization protocol). (Specify evaluation procedure and schedule.)

Short-term Objective 3: Given a color-coded story board and accompanying pictures, Student will reformulate a story that has just been read to her, by placing the pictures on the story board in the appropriate sequence, incorporating the elements of *character*, *setting*, *time*, and *activities*, across (specify number) different stories, (specify criteria) given, (specify prompt levels/fade back plan and generalization protocol). (Specify evaluation procedure and schedule.)

Short-term Objective 4: Given accompanying manual signs and *indirect* verbal cues, Student will verbally retell a story in the appropriate time sequence, incorporating the elements of *character, setting, time*, and *activities* across (specify number) different stories, (specify criteria) given (specify prompt levels/fade back plan and generalization protocol). (Specify evaluation procedure and schedule.)

Recommended Educational Programming Formats:
A, B, E, F, G, H, K, L, M, Q

CONTENT AREA:
Sentence Formulation

Sample PLP for an 8-year-old student with HFA: *Student is a verbal child who will often initiate interactions with others. Formal testing and informal assessment indicate, however, that Student has significant difficulties with sentence formulation. Specifically, when asked a question, Student will often pantomime his response. When cued to use words, he will either give a one-word response, or say that he doesn't know the answer. When Student initiates language, his speech is characterized by multiple grammatical errors and difficulty with word order. These problems affect his ability to participate effectively in the classroom curriculum, and adversely affect his relationships with peers.*

Goal/Objective Templates Based upon PLP:

Annual Goal: Student will demonstrate improvement in formulating sentences as specified in, and measured by short-term objectives.

Short-term Objective 1: Given a color-coded visual template for subject, verb, and object, and direct instruction in its use, Student will produce sentences of (specify number e.g., 5) words in length, in the correct order, (specify criteria) given (specify prompt levels/fade back plan and generalization protocol). (Specify evaluation procedure and schedule.)

Short-term Objective 2: Given a visual template for subject, verb, and object, Student will expand his sentence length from (specify number e.g., 5 words to 7 words), producing them in the correct order, (specify criteria) given (specify prompt levels/fade back plan and generalization protocol). (Specify evaluation procedure and schedule.)

Recommended Educational Programming Formats: A, C, F, H, J, K, L, M, N, O, Q

CONTENT AREA:
Word Retrieval

Sample PLP for a 13-year-old student with HFA: *Student possesses strengths in both vocabulary development and reading decoding. While her performance on the Expressive One-Word Picture Vocabulary Test—Revised (EOWPVT—R) is within normal limits, both her teachers and parents report that she manifests word retrieval difficulty "in the heat of the cognitively demanding moment." This problem makes it difficult for Student to answer questions in a timely manner in class. It also affects her ability to answer written test questions across subjects in her inclusive classroom and resource room settings.*

Goal/Objective Templates Based upon PLP:

Annual Goal: Student will demonstrate improvement in word retrieval as specified in, and measured by short-term objectives.

Short-term Objective 1: Given a set of pictures depicting common objects, Student will name (specify number) pictures in a period of (specify number) seconds/minutes, (specify criteria) given (specify prompt levels/fade back plan and generalization protocol). (Specify evaluation procedure and schedule.)

Explanatory notes:

- Naming pictures in a strict, timed format is known as *confrontation naming*. It is a technique used by speech-language pathologists to provide practice in word retrieval. Naming drills are typically delivered within a discrete trial format, in rapid-fire fashion, using flash cards.

- Depending upon student progress, this objective can be adjusted for number of pictures presented, and amount of time allotted for naming.

• A large number of pictures should be continually recycled throughout the year in order to provide a great deal of practice in confrontation naming.

Short-term Objective 2: Given manual sign cues or cloze sentences, as needed, Student will demonstrate the ability to retrieve words in actual classroom settings by providing the appropriate answer in response to questions, (specify criteria and generalization protocol). (Specify evaluation procedure and schedule.)

Explanatory note: No additional prompts are needed, since the underlying conditions serve as the ultimate cues for performance.

Recommended Educational Programming Formats: A, G, H, K, L, M, O, Q

CONTENT AREA:
Oral-Motor Skills—Oral Sensitivity

**Sample PLP for a 5-year-old student with moderate
autism and severe oral-motor difficulty:** *Although the
number of foods and other types of oral stimuli that Student
will tolerate has increased this year, the number of foods that he
will sample is, nonetheless, very restricted. According to clinical
observation and teacher report, he prefers crunchy foods, and
needs multiple cues to attempt to eat semi-solid foods such as
applesauce. He is clearly resistant to exploring any type of oral
stimuli. In addition, oral sensitivity issues impact Student's
ability to produce the oral movements necessary for speech production, leaving him with only primitive and/or aberrant
means of communicating his needs. These difficulties compromise his ability to function appropriately in his kindergarten
classroom.*

Goal/Objective Templates Based upon PLP:

Annual Goal: Student will demonstrate increased tolerance
for oral stimuli as specified in, and measured by short-term
objectives.

Short-term Objective 1: Given a variety of tastes, temperatures, and textures of oral materials (e.g., foods, oral-motor
toys, face cloths, etc.) Student will demonstrate increased
tolerance for oral stimuli by allowing these items into the
proximity of the (specify area, e.g., lips, tongue, etc.), (specify criteria) given (specify prompt levels/fade back plan and
generalization protocol). (Specify evaluation procedure and
schedule.)

Explanatory note: Work on this objective should generate a
group of oral materials that the student can tolerate reasonably well. These can be used with the next objective.

Short-term Objective 2: Given a variety of oral materials that Student will tolerate in proximity to the (specify area e.g., lips, tongue, etc.), he will demonstrate increased tolerance for them by exploring them for gradually increasing periods of time (e.g., 30 seconds, 1 minute, 2 minutes, etc.), (specify criteria e.g., 3/5 opportunities across 3/5 days) given (specify prompt levels/fade back plan and generalization protocol). (Specify evaluation procedure and schedule.)

Recommended Educational Programming Formats: A, K, L, M, Q

CONTENT AREA:
Oral-Motor Skills—Oral-Motor Planning

Sample PLP for a 4-year-old student with moderate autism and severe oral-motor difficulty: *By parent report and teacher observation, Student is able to say words more easily when she is excited or angry. She also is beginning to say the alphabet (albeit inarticulately), having learned it from an alphabet song. When she is asked to repeat words or letters outside the context of the song, she has great difficulty repeating them. Her speech-language pathologist reports that informal assessment has revealed that Student has difficulty producing voluntary movements, and that she appears to be dyspraxic (i.e., has difficulty with oral-motor planning for speech purposes). While Student enjoys it when her teachers utilize oral-motor tools such as whistles, she does not attempt to operate them herself. Further, although she enjoys watching bubbles when someone else blows them, when the bubble wand is held up to her mouth she will either move her head toward it, or attempt to lick it. She is also becoming quite resistant to "anything that involves her mouth," according to her mother. Student's problems with oral-motor planning interfere with her ability to produce the oral movements necessary for speech production. They also adversely affect her ability to participate in several of the activities within her preschool classroom.*

Goal/Objective Templates Based upon PLP:

Annual Goal: Student will demonstrate improvement in producing voluntary oral movements as specified in, and measured by short-term objectives.

Short-term Objective 1: Given a variety of oral-motor tools (e.g., whistles, bubble wand, straws, etc.) Student will perform the oral movements necessary to cause (specify number e.g. 2, 5, etc.) different tools to function in the manner intended, (specify criteria) given (specify prompt levels/fade back plan and generalization protocol). (Specify evaluation procedure and schedule.)

Short-term Objective 2: Given a variety of songs, chants, and nursery rhymes that Student finds motivating, she will demonstrate improved oral-motor functioning by gradually improving her production of words, (specify criteria e.g., rating scale) given (specify prompt levels/fade back plan and generalization protocol). (Specify evaluation procedure and schedule.)

Recommended Educational Programming Formats: A, D, K, L, M, Q

CONTENT AREA:
Oral-Motor Skills—Sound/Speech Production

Sample PLP for a 3-year-old student with autism and severe oral-motor difficulty: *According to clinical observation and informal assessment, Student frequently engages in vocal play/babbling, but he does not yet imitate others' vocalizations, nor does he play vocal games when others imitate him. His speech-language pathologist reports that Student is at an emerging stage of imitative development, and that he is beginning to exhibit the oral-motor control necessary to imitate others' vocalizations. Student's difficulties impact his ability to produce sounds on a voluntary basis for speech production. They also negatively impact his ability to make his needs known both at home and in school.*

Goal/Objective Templates Based upon PLP:

Annual Goal: Student will demonstrate improvement in producing voluntary sounds/vocalizations as specified in, and measured by short-term objectives.

Short-term Objective 1: Given extensive vocal input presented in a game-like format, Student will engage in vocal play with others when adults imitate his vocalizations, for (specify number e.g., 3, 4) turns, (specify criteria, including level of consistency e.g., 3/5 days) (specify generalization protocol). (Specify evaluation procedure and schedule.)

Explanatory notes:

- Prompt levels do not need to be specified, since cues are incorporated into the underlying condition.

- Additional prompts would likely negatively impact the automaticity of vocal play by calling attention to oral structures.

Short-term Objective 2: Given a pause in a familiar song/ nursery rhyme to capitalize on automaticity, Student will make a sound to fill in the blank, (specify criteria) given (specify prompt levels/fade back plan [e.g., phonemic cue, expectant waiting], and generalization protocol). (Specify evaluation procedure and schedule.)

Recommended Educational Programming Formats: A, C, D, K, L, M, Q

Sample PLP for a 4-year-old student with moderate autism and severe oral-motor difficulty: *Student will often attempt to communicate verbally, but her teacher and parents report that they have difficulty understanding her. Informal assessment indicates that even though Student's vocal imitation skills have improved greatly this year, she still presents with a limited sound repertoire. She also needs tactile and other multi-sensory cues to produce many sounds. She can currently produce the consonants: /p/, /b/, /k/, /g/, /n/, and /d/ and the vowels: "ee," "ai," "oo," and "o" with a model, alone. In natural situations, she tends to use only the consonants /n/ and /d/. These difficulties impact Student's ability to produce functional speech, and to participate in activities within the preschool classroom.*

Goal/Objective Templates Based upon PLP:

Annual Goal: Student will demonstrate improvement in using sounds in functional activities as specified in, and measured by short-term objectives.

Short-term Objective 1: Given vocal models, toy props (e.g., car/truck), and multi-sensory cues, Student will produce (specify number) different sounds across (specify

number) facilitated play activities, (specify criteria and fade
back plan for multi-sensory cues, and generalization protocol). (Specify evaluation procedure and schedule.)

Explanatory note: Since the multi-sensory cues serve as
both the underlying condition and the prompt, it is not necessary to specify other prompts.

Short-term Objective 2: Given (specify number) children's
songs (e.g., *Old MacDonald Had A Farm*) and (specify
number) nursery rhymes (e.g., *Baa Baa Black Sheep*),
Student will produce selected sounds in context (e.g., *"E I E
I O"* and *baa baa*, respectively), (specify criteria) given (specify prompt levels/fade back plan and generalization
protocol). (Specify evaluation procedure and schedule.)

Recommended Educational Programming Formats:
A, C, D, F, K, L, M, O, Q

**Sample PLP for an 8-year-old student with autism and
moderate-severe oral-motor difficulty:** *While Student will
frequently verbally attempt to communicate with others, her
speech is characterized by multiple articulation errors.
Student's speech-language pathologist reports that informal
assessment indicates that Student presents with symptoms of
dyspraxia (i.e., oral-motor planning difficulty) affecting her
ability to sequence and correctly pronounce sounds and words.
Intensive oral-motor therapy has resulted in some gains;
however, these have not typically been observed in day-to-day
speech. Thus, a more functional approach to improving speech
production is needed to allow her to more effectively use the
words and phrases that she is attempting to say in her classroom
and home environments. These difficulties impact Student's
ability to communicate effectively across settings, and cause
her a great deal of frustration, as well.*

Goal/Objective Templates Based upon PLP:

Annual Goal: Student will demonstrate improvement in speech production as specified in, and measured by short-term objectives.

Short-term Objective 1: Given multi-sensory cues, Student will produce (specify number, e.g., 10, 15) functional words/phrases in contrived situations with an *informed* listener, (specify criteria, e.g. rating scale level, and fade back plan for multi-sensory cues). (Specify generalization protocol and evaluation procedure and schedule).

Explanatory notes:

- Since the multi-sensory cues serve as both the underlying condition and the prompt, it is not necessary to specify other prompts.
- Rating scale may specify such elements as: correct number of syllables; correct sequence of syllables; correct consonant and/or vowel production, etc.

Short-term Objective 2: Given prior practice, Student will produce (specify number) functional words/phrases in (specify number) natural situations across (specify number) *novel* listeners, (specify criteria, e.g. rating scale level) given (specify prompt levels/fade back plan). (Specify evaluation procedure and schedule.)

Explanatory note: The generalization protocol does not need to be specified, since it is already built into the objective.

Recommended Educational Programming Formats: A, B, C, F, J, K, L, M, O, Q

Miscellaneous Short-Term Objective Templates for Communication and Expression

Short-term Objective 1: Given accompanying manual sign cues, Student will provide information related to the social-emotional domain for characters in his/her reading book in response to (specify number) specific questions, (specify criteria) given (specify prompt levels/fade back plan and generalization protocol). (Specify evaluation procedure and schedule.)

Short-term Objective 2: Given direct instruction in (specify number) common social phrases (e.g., *"I got it"; "Your turn"*, etc.), and manual sign cues, Student will apply these phrases in contextually appropriate activities in role-play situations with 1 peer, (specify criteria) given (specify prompt levels/fade back plan and generalization protocol). (Specify evaluation procedure and schedule.)

Short-term Objective 3: Given an array of (specify number) small stationary objects (e.g., "doll house" table, bed, chair, etc.), Student will verbally direct a peer to place (specify number) other moveable objects (e.g., shoe, doll, apple, etc.) in various places vis-à-vis the stationary items (e.g., *in, on, under,* etc.) in a barrier game activity, (specify criteria) given (specify prompt levels/fade back plan and generalization protocol). (Specify evaluation procedure and schedule.)

Short-term Objective 4: Given a variety of objects, pictures, and/or activities that Student finds motivating, Student will share attention with another individual, as demonstrated by one or more of the following:

• Eye gaze/exchange of eye contact/gaze shifts

• Pointing/offering/extending

• Responding physically to the actions/directives of others (e.g., performing tasks/activities).

(Specify criteria) given (specify prompt levels/fade back plan and generalization protocol). (Specify evaluation procedure and schedule.)

Short-term Objective 5: Given accompanying manual sign cues, Student will employ the particular pragmatic function of communication (e.g., *obtaining attention, requesting, protesting, asking questions,* etc.) that is appropriate to the situation, event, or activity, (specify criteria) given (specify prompt levels/fade back plan and generalization protocol). (Specify evaluation procedure and schedule.)

Explanatory notes:

- Objective 5 is comprehensive by design, since it targets the *use* of several pragmatic functions in context.

- Specific times of the week can be set aside to probe the pragmatic areas listed in the objective to derive meaningful data over time and activities/events.

- This objective, as worded, is ideal for promoting generalization across activities, people, and referents.

General Teaching Tips & Strategies for Communication, Expression, and Oral-Motor Skills

1. Set up/structure situations to encourage communication. Some examples:

   - Snack time (wait for the student to request; give small portions; wait for the student to obtain your attention, etc.)

   - Place needed/desired items out of reach (e.g. glue, crayons, a favorite toy, etc.) so that the student has a reason to communicate.

   - Offer the student things that you know he/she doesn't like to elicit an appropriate protest.

   - Skip a desired part of a well-known routine, so that the student has a reason and opportunity to supply needed information.

   - Provide activities that are interesting and motivating *to the student* to facilitate spontaneous commenting.

   - Increase salience wherever and whenever possible (e.g., Use color to highlight information. Make things "larger than life.").

   - Bring in a motivating toy, pet, or interesting object to provide both an impetus and context for communication/expression.

   - "Misunderstand"/"play dumb" to create a *need* to communicate.

   - *Follow the student's lead in terms of his/her interests.*

2. Use referential communication tasks (i.e., barrier games) to demonstrate and teach the power of communication in a motivating context. These can be designed by speech-language pathologists, and are excellent vehicles

177

for use in speech-language therapy and social, play, and leisure activities.

3. Use demonstration and modeling of target responses (e.g., nonverbal behavior, words, and phrases) whenever possible so that student has a model of the behavior desired.

4. Utilize visual supports such as sign language and sentence strips to facilitate the use of longer, more sophisticated utterances.

5. Give the student access to a variety of means of communication that he/she can use to *initiate* interactions.

6. Use manual signs to help facilitate both word retrieval and sentence expansion.

7. Provide students with multi-modal language input/ feedback including, but not limited to the use of natural gestures, manual signs, pictures, written words, etc., since they help to facilitate comprehension which is the basis for *meaningful* expression. Moreover, repeated exposure to the model, over time, can help to improve speech production.

8. Begin all oral-motor sessions with an oral-motor "warm-up." The purpose of the warm-up is to prepare students for speech therapy and other oral-motor work.* The warm-up activities should involve allowing the student to experience a variety of tastes, temperatures, and textures in and around the face and mouth. *Whether materials are edible or inedible, they should be monitored at all times so that oral stimulation is provided safely.*

9. Strive to make oral-motor activities as pleasurable as possible, and try to utilize techniques to take the student's attention away from his/her mouth and the act of speaking.* Helpful strategies/activities include:

- Using cloze sentences (e.g. *"Ready, set,..." "There is someone at the ..."*)

- Combining speech with motor movements (e.g. *"Jump, jump, jump,"* as the student is performing the act)

- Singing songs about what the student is doing

- Using rhythmic and rhyming activities, in general

10. Depending upon the nature of the oral-motor difficulty, some of the more resistant oral-motor problems may respond to the use of more intrusive and/or multiple cues to facilitate correct production of sounds and words.* These activities can include:

- Mirror work

- Touch/tactile cues

- Physical manipulation of oral structures

*Note: *Oral-motor therapy activities should only be conducted by, or under the strict supervision of, a certified or licensed speech-language pathologist (e.g. strategies 8–10), or a registered/licensed occupational therapist (e.g. strategy 8.)*

Useful Teaching Resources

(See *Appendix B* for additional information.)

1. *Can-Do Oral-Motor Fun and Games.* By J. P. DeNinno & K. A. Gill.

2. *Dyspraxia: A Guide for Teachers and Parents.* By K. Ripley, B. Daines, & J. Barrett.

3. *Early Communication Skills.* By C. Lynch & J. Kidd.

4. *Expanding and Combining Sentences.* By M. M. Toomey.

5. *Explaining.* By M. M. Toomey.

6. *Great Therapy Ideas! Oral Sensory-Motor Tool-Toys Techniques.* By C. Boshart, H. Demetrion, C. Haislip, T. Harrison, J. Jared, L. Kelly, M. Schueller, & T. Szypulski.

7. *Listening, Understanding, Remembering, Verbalizing!* By J. G. DeGaetano.

8. *Mouth Madness: Oral-Motor Activities for Children.* By C. Orr.

9. *Narrative Toolbox: Blueprints for Storybuilding.* By P. Hudson-Nechkash.

10. *Oral-Motor Activities for Young Children.* By E. Mackie.

11. *Oral-Motor Techniques in Articulation and Phonological Therapy.* By P. Marshalla.

12. *Teaching Spontaneous Communication to Autistic and Developmentally Handicapped Children.* By L. R. Watson, C. Lord, B. Schaffer, & E. Schopler.

13. *Teaching Your Child the Language of Social Success.* By M. Duke, S. Nowicki & E. Martin.

14. *Telling A Story.* By M. M. Toomey.

15. *This Is the One That I Want.* By L.G. Richman.

16. *Understanding the Nature of Autism: A Practical Guide.* By J. Janzen.

17. *Visual Strategies for Improving Communication.* By L. Hodgdon.

Chapter 13

Sample IEP Goal and Objective Templates for Social Interaction, Play, and Leisure Skills

Rationale for Inclusion of This Skill Category:

- Impairment in social understanding and interaction is not only one of the most commonly recognized areas of disability in students with ASD, but also one of its hallmark features.

- Research demonstrates that children with autism present with deficits in the development of imagination (Peeters & Gillberg, 1999; Twachtman-Cullen, 2000a) and symbolic play (Wolfberg, 1999).

- Social interaction skills are crucial to the development of communicative competence (Kaye, 1982).

- Older students with ASD often have difficulty knowing what to do during unstructured leisure time or work breaks.

Present Levels of Performance for Social Interaction, Play, and Leisure Skills Should Include:

- A statement indicating the student's strengths in areas of social interaction and/or play/leisure skills. If addressing play, it is helpful to include the child's level of play skills development (e.g., *solitary, parallel, associative*, etc.).

- A statement regarding the student's weaknesses in specific areas of social interaction and/or play/leisure skills, particularly as they relate to *priority* educational needs for the coming year.

- A statement of how the student's disability in the areas of social interaction and/or play/leisure skills impacts his/her involvement and progress in the general curriculum (or, for preschool children, in appropriate activities).

- The source(s) of the statement(s) in the PLP.

- Any additional information that can enable the PLP to fulfill its two important functions: 1) *To serve as the basis for generating need-based, individualized IEP objectives;* and, 2) *To serve as the standard by which to judge performance/ progress.*

CONTENT AREA:
Social Interaction—Responding/Social Reciprocity

Sample PLP for a 4-year-old student with severe autism and mental retardation: *According to informal assessment and parent report, Student presents with pragmatic skills that cluster in the 3–6 month range. He demonstrates severe difficulties in responding to others socially, and in using his skills to communicate his needs. For example, student rarely makes eye contact during requests or other interactive situations to indicate awareness of the social nature of such activities. According to his teacher, he is most attentive to others when favorite songs are sung. In addition, he is beginning to enjoy mirror play. These difficulties impact his ability to participate in activities in his preschool program, particularly those involving social interactions.*

Goal/Objective Templates Based upon PLP:

Annual Goal: Student will demonstrate improvement in social interaction as specified in, and measured by short-term objectives.

Short-term Objective 1: Given developmentally appropriate and motivating activities, Student will demonstrate improvement in reciprocal social behaviors by responding with (specify response e.g., eye contact and/or positive affect) to a social game (e.g., *Pat-a-cake; Peek-a-boo,* etc.) with an adult, (specify criteria for both length of time e.g., 2 turns, 30 seconds, 4/5 opportunities, etc.; and consistency e.g., 4/5 days), given (specify prompt levels/fade back plan and generalization protocol). (Specify evaluation procedure and schedule.)

Short-term Objective 2: Given developmentally appropriate, motivating activities, and a means of requesting (i.e.,

185

small representational object or picture), Student will *initiate* (specify number) familiar social game(s) with (specify person e.g., the clinician, peer), (specify criteria e.g., length of interaction; consistency over time). (Specify generalization protocol and evaluation procedure and schedule.)

Explanatory note: In Objective 2, specification of prompt levels is not necessary since the student is expected to *initiate* the interaction.

Recommended Educational Programming Formats: A, C, D, F, K, L, M, O, Q

CONTENT AREA:
Social Interaction—Basic Turn-Taking

Sample PLP for a 5-year-old student with severe autism: *According to clinical observation and teacher report, Student is able to entertain herself for long periods of time when she is involved in activities of her own choosing. In addition, when given a choice of activities, Student always chooses to play by herself. She actively avoids contact with adults and peers, particularly in the context of social interaction and play. Student's speech-language pathologist reports that she seems to lack understanding of the reciprocal nature of communication. Specifically, she will lead others to desired objects, but will rarely make eye contact with them. Thus, she uses the hand of the individual as a tool rather than recognizes the person as a social interactant. These difficulties impact her ability to participate in group and play activities within her preschool classroom.*

Goal/Objective Templates Based upon PLP:

Annual Goal: Student will demonstrate improvement in two-way social interaction as specified in, and measured by short-term objectives.

Short-term Objective 1: Given gestural and manual sign support (e.g., *my turn/your turn*; physically passing a toy from adult to student and vice versa), Student will fill her turn (specify number e.g., 3, 4) times in a play interaction with an *adult* involving a familiar toy, (specify criteria) given (specify prompt levels/fade back plan and generalization protocol). (Specify evaluation procedure and schedule.)

Short-term Objective 2: Given gestural and manual sign support (e.g., *my turn/your turn*) Student will fill her turn (specify number e.g., 3, 4) times in a play interaction with a *peer* involving a familiar toy, (specify criteria) given (specify

187

prompt levels/fade back plan and generalization protocol). (Specify evaluation procedure and schedule.)

Explanatory notes:

- Activities could include:

  - Rolling a ball, car, etc. back and forth

  - Performing a *concrete* action on a toy (e.g. putting shapes into a shape sorter, pushing a button on a toy to activate it, etc.)

- Progress on this objective would be evidenced by the length of time the child is engaged in the interaction, the number of turns that the child is able to take, and the consistency with which he/she can maintain such interactions over time.

- The above-noted indications of progress may be incorporated into the objectives cited previously, or, if the IEP team so chooses, separate objectives could be written to reflect this information.

Recommended Educational Programming Formats: A, C, E, F, K, L, M, O, Q

CONTENT AREA:
Play Skills Development

Sample PLP for a 6-year-old student with autism:
*According to parents and teacher, once Student is interested in
a particular toy, he can derive enjoyment from it. They state,
however, that he is very resistant to new things. When left to his
own devices, he will often engage in self-stimulatory behavior
with toys. He particularly likes shiny objects, and will often hold
them up to his eyes. He also spins the wheels on toy cars. In addition, Student will only attempt to play with two of the items in
the play corner, and protests when presented with any other
object. These difficulties impact Student's ability to learn about
the characteristics of objects and the relationships between
objects and events in his special education setting and in mainstream experiences, as well. They also impact his ability to derive
benefit from typical peers.*

Goal/Objective Templates Based Upon PLP:

Annual Goal: Student will expand his toy play as specified
in, and measured by short-term objectives.

Short-term Objective 1: Given (specify number e.g., 2, 3)
new toys that contain elements of interest to the student
(e.g., *shiny*, or with components that *spin*), Student will
incorporate at least (specify number e.g., 1, 2) actions into
his toy play, (specify criteria) given (specify prompt levels/
fade back plan and generalization protocol). (Specify evaluation procedure and schedule.)

Short-term Objective 2: Given (specify number e.g., 2, 3)
new toys that contain elements of interest to the student
(e.g., *shiny*, or with components that *spin*), and demonstra-
tion/modeling of actions within a simple play scenario,
Student will incorporate at least (specify number) actions
into his own play scenario (specify criteria) given (specify

prompt levels/fade back plan and generalization protocol). (Specify evaluation procedure and schedule.)

Recommended Educational Programming Formats: A, C, K, L, M, O, Q

CONTENT AREA:
Play Skills Development—Using Social Scripts

Sample PLP for a 5-year-old student with AS: *Student is
extremely verbal with adults, particularly if talking about
trains—his current abiding interest. His parents have expressed
concern, however, because when they take him to the park or to
visit other children, he shows no interest whatsoever in what they
are doing or saying. Attempts to get him to join in games have
been met with a great deal of resistance. These difficulties prevent Student from participating fully in kindergarten activities
with peers.*

Goal/Objective Templates Based Upon PLP:

Annual Goal: Student will demonstrate increased play interactions with peers as specified in, and measured by
short-term objective(s).

Short-term Objective: Given a social script involving a pre-
tend train trip, rules for playing, props, and assigned roles,
Student will select a role and perform the actions required,
with at least (specify number e.g., 3, 4) peers across (specify
number) days per month (specify criteria e.g., for gradually
increasing periods of time) given (specify prompt levels/fade
back plan and generalization protocol). (Specify evaluation
procedure and schedule.)

Explanatory notes:

- Since this child has an "abiding interest" in trains, the
  selection of the above-noted play scenario provides a
  highly motivating activity in which he can interact with
  other children and practice play skills.

- Other "abiding interests" may be substituted to meet the
  individual needs of other students.

Recommended Educational Programming Formats:
C, D, E, F, L, N, Q

CONTENT AREA:
Play Skills Development—Interactive Play

Sample PLP for a 4-year-old student with PDD-NOS:
According to both formal and informal testing, Student manifests strengths in academic areas such as knowing her colors, shapes, and numbers. She is extremely active, and reportedly "flits" from thing to thing. Her parents report that she enjoys "rough-house" play, and other high-intensity activities. Attempts to get her to interact with other children in the preschool classroom have not been successful, and have compromised her success in that setting.

Goal/Objective Templates Based Upon PLP:

Annual Goal: Student will demonstrate improvement in interactive play with peers as specified in, and measured by short-term objectives.

Short-term Objective 1: Given motivating, developmentally appropriate high intensity activities, Student will engage in reciprocal play interactions with at least (specify number) peer(s) by performing the actions appropriate to the activity, (specify criteria) given (specify prompt levels/fade back plan and generalization protocol). (Specify evaluation procedure and schedule.)

Explanatory note: High intensity activities can include the following: playing *Ring-Around-the-Rosie; Row, Row, Row Your Boat* with a partner; seesaw interactions; playing *London Bridge,* and similar activities.

Short-term Objective 2: Given motivating nursery rhymes (e.g., *Jack Be Nimble; Jack and Jill,* etc.) demonstration, and modeling, Student will act out a particular part in a role-play activity with at least (specify number) peer(s) across (specify number) nursery rhymes, (specify criteria) given (specify

prompt levels/fade back plan and generalization protocol).
(Specify evaluation procedure and schedule.)

Recommended Educational Programming Formats:
A, C, D, F, L, M, N, Q

CONTENT AREA:
Leisure Skill Development

Sample PLP for a 16-year-old student with moderate autism: *Student works very hard in both his highly structured vocational class and job site. He has difficulty, however, during unstructured time, (i.e., the 15-minute break that he is required to take). His parents also report that Student becomes agitated and restless when he is at home and time is not structured for him. These difficulties impact his ability to function effectively across home, school, and work settings.*

Goal/Objective Templates Based Upon PLP:

Annual Goal: Student will participate in a functional leisure routine as specified in, and measured by short-term objective(s).

Explanatory note: It is recommended that an ecological inventory be taken in order to develop a list of leisure activities that the student finds pleasurable.

Short-term Objective: Given a group of leisure activities that the student finds pleasurable, he will choose an activity from a visual array of (specify number) choices, and participate in it, (specify criteria e.g., for gradually increasing periods of time) given (specify prompt levels/fade back plan and generalization protocol). (Specify evaluation procedure and schedule.)

Recommended Educational Programming Formats: A, C, K, L, O, P, Q

194

Content Area:
Following Social Rules/
"Sizing Up" Social Situations

Sample PLP for a 15-year-old student with AS: *Student is described as "very social" by her parents and teacher. Despite this, her lack of knowledge of the "unwritten rules" of social discourse can impede her ability to interact with others appropriately. When conversing, she is frequently observed to stand too close to adults and peers. This causes a good deal of discomfort to peers, in particular, and has resulted in some of them avoiding interactions with Student. These difficulties impact Student's ability to establish relationships with peers and to effectively function in her classroom and vocational settings.*

Goal/Objective Template Based Upon PLP:

Annual Goal: Student will demonstrate improvement in the maintenance of appropriate social distance in social interactive situations as specified in, and measured by short-term objective(s).

Short-term Objective: Given direct instruction, and visual supports (e.g., tape on the floor; outstretched arm), Student will maintain an appropriate social distance when speaking to another person for gradually increasing periods of time from (specify time, e.g., 3–7 minutes), (specify criteria) given (specify prompt levels/fade back plan and generalization protocol). (Specify evaluation procedure and schedule.)

Recommended Educational Programming Formats:
A, B, C, L, N, O, P, Q

Sample PLP for a 10-year-old student with PDD-NOS:
According to his teacher, Student appears motivated to interact with peers, as judged by his frequent attempts to interact in the classroom setting. Despite his interest in peer interaction, however, he is unsuccessful in these attempts. His difficulty appears to stem from a lack of social understanding, as judged by his problems in "reading" social situations. These difficulties are reportedly off-putting to his peers, and hence negatively impact Student's ability to derive benefit from typical peer models in his inclusive classroom setting.

Annual Goal: Student will demonstrate improvement in understanding social situations as specified in, and measured by short-term objectives.

Short-term Objective 1: Given direct instruction, exaggerated cues, and observational vignettes, Student will "size up" a variety of social situations by selecting appropriate explanations of them within a multiple choice format, (specify criteria) given (specify prompt levels/fade back plan and generalization protocol). (Specify evaluation procedure and schedule.)

Short-term Objective 2: Given *indirect* cues and observational vignettes, Student will "size up" a variety of social situations by providing verbal explanations of them, (specify criteria) given (specify prompt levels/fade back plan and generalization protocol). (Specify evaluation procedure and schedule.)

Short-term Objective 3: Given indirect cues, and manual signs, as needed, Student will demonstrate social understanding by generating appropriate social responses in contextually relevant role play situations, (specify criteria) given (specify prompt levels/fade back plan and generalization protocol). (Specify evaluation procedure and schedule.)

Short-term Objective 4: Given visual supports (e.g., *Social Stories)* for a given social context, Student will demonstrate his understanding of social information/events by exhibiting social behavior appropriate to the context, (specify criteria) given (specify prompt levels/fade back plan and generalization protocol). (Specify evaluation procedure and schedule.)

Explanatory note: For additional information on *Social Stories* (Gray, 1994/2000), see *Appendix B.*

Recommended Educational Programming Formats: A, B, C, K, L, M, N, O, Q

CONTENT AREA:
Social Interactive Games

Sample PLP for an 8-year-old student with PDD-NOS:
Student enjoys playing card and board games with others. Clinical observation and teacher report indicate, however, that she has difficulty understanding when it is her turn and when she must give peers a turn in the game. This is particularly problematic in games where there are double turns, or where one must miss a turn. This behavior frustrates her peers and interferes with Student's ability to develop social relationships in her classroom.

Goal/Objective Templates Based Upon PLP:

Annual Goal: Student will demonstrate improvement in taking turns in games as specified in, and measured by short-term objectives.

Short-term Objective 1: Given direct instruction and the initial use of a turn marker (e.g., a circle with the words *My turn* written on it), Student will take turns with a peer in a game-playing situation by moving the turn marker back and forth at the appropriate times, (specify criteria) given (specify prompt levels/fade back plan and generalization protocol). (Specify evaluation procedure and schedule.)

Short-term Objective 2: Given accompanying manual signs and gestures, Student will take turns with a peer for a gradually increasing number of turns, (specify criteria) given (specify prompt levels/fade back plan and generalization protocol). (Specify evaluation procedure and schedule.)

Recommended Educational Programming Formats: C, E, F, L, M, O, Q

Miscellaneous Short-Term Objective Templates for Social Interaction, Play, and Leisure Skills

Short-term Objective 1: Given a variety of activities and events that Student finds enjoyable/motivating, he/she will demonstrate engagement by generating an affective response appropriate to the situation (e.g., smiles, eye contact, gaze shifts, etc.), (specify criteria) given (specify prompt levels/ fade back plan and generalization protocol). (Specify evaluation procedure and schedule.)

Short-term Objective 2: Given a sand- or water-table, and a variety of containers, Student will demonstrate his/her comfort level in the proximity of peers by playing in parallel fashion alongside (specify number) peers, (specify criteria e.g., for gradually increasing periods of time; across 3/5 days) given (specify prompt levels/fade back plan and generalization protocol). (Specify evaluation procedure and schedule.)

Short-term Objective 3: Given a sand- or water-table, and a variety of containers, Student will demonstrate associative play skills by handing items to, and accepting them from (specify number) peers, (specify criteria e.g., increase in the number of times the behavior is exhibited or the length of time the child is engaged in the activity; consistency of interactions over time) given (specify prompt levels/fade back plan and generalization protocol). (Specify evaluation procedure and schedule.)

Short-term Objective 4: Given direct instruction in "small talk" activities, examples, and modeling, Student will carry on a conversation across (specify number) small talk topics (e.g., discussion about the weather—*if it is not the student's abiding interest*; discussion about a television program; what Student had for breakfast, etc.) in structured role plays with a peer, (specify criteria e.g., across 3, 4, etc. conversational turns) given (specify prompt levels/fade back plan and generalization protocol). (Specify evaluation procedure and schedule.)

General Teaching Tips & Strategies For Social Interaction, Play, & Leisure Skills

1. Utilize motivating, developmentally appropriate toys (for younger students), and developmentally appropriate activities (for older students).

2. Work within functional, naturalistic contexts whenever possible, to help facilitate the generalization of skills.

3. Provide direct instruction to students, utilizing demonstration and modeling, whenever possible.

4. Provide visual supports to accompany language input, as well as hand-over-hand assistance *only* when it is necessary for successful performance.

5. Keep uppermost in mind that play and leisure skills must be *enjoyable* to the student if they are to qualify under the category of *play* and *leisure*. "Forcing" enjoyment, because it happens to be "time for play," distorts the properties of play and leisure.

6. Repetition of social, play, and leisure activities over time is critical both to *learning* and *generalizing* these important skills.

7. Train paraprofessionals to work on social, play, and leisure skills in classroom, recess, resource room, and extra-curricular settings to promote generalization.

8. Concretize the abstract concept of turn taking by using a turn marker (e.g., circle with the words *My turn* written on it).

9. Provide much needed social interaction practice for students in non-threatening environments through the use of structured role-plays.

10. Consider using the following educational supports, as they are very helpful to students with ASD:

- *Social Stories* (Gray, 1994/2000)
- *Comic Strip Conversations* (Gray, 1994)
- Social scripts
- Lists of social rules
- Social sequence templates
- Joint activity play routines

Useful Teaching Resources

(See *Appendix B* for additional information.)

1. *Comic Strip Conversations.* By C. Gray.

2. *Early Communication Skills.* By C. Lynch & J. Kidd.

3. *Helping the Child Who Doesn't Fit In.* By S. Nowicki Jr. & M. P. Duke.

4. *How To Be A Para Pro: A Comprehensive Training Manual For Paraprofessionals.* By D. Twachtman-Cullen.

5. *More Social Skills Stories: Very Personal Picture Stories for Readers and Nonreaders K–12.* By A.M. Johnson.

6. *New Social Stories Illustrated.* By C. Gray.

7. *Play and Imagination in Children with Autism.* By P. J. Wolfberg.

8. *Social Skills Activities for Special Children.* By D. Mannix.

9. *Social Skills Stories: Functional Picture Stories for Readers and Nonreaders K–12.* By A. M. Johnson & J. L. Susnik.

10. *Social Skill Strategies: A Social-Emotional Curriculum for Adolescents* (Book A). By N. Gajewski, P. Hirn, & P. Mayo.

11. *Teaching Your Child the Language of Social Success.* By M. Duke, S. Nowicki, & E. Martin.

12. *Understanding the Nature of Autism: A Practical Guide.* By J. Janzen.

13. *Visual Strategies for Improving Communication.* By L. Hodgdon.

Chapter 14

Sample IEP Goal and Objective Templates for Cognitive and Social-Cognitive Skills

Rationale for Inclusion of this Skill Category:

- According to several research studies, individuals with ASD present with deficits in *executive function* (EF) skills (Ozonoff, 1997; Pennington, Bennetto, McAleer, & Roberts, 1996). EF skills encompass the following areas of functioning:

    - Mental planning
    - Set maintenance (i.e., the ability to keep one's mind on what one is doing)
    - Impulse control
    - Flexibility in thought and action

- Ability to keep plans/goals "on line" (i.e., in working memory)
- Self-monitoring

• Deficits in EF negatively impact organizational ability, time management, and planning.

• Research demonstrates that individuals with ASD present with deficits in *critical thinking* (Minshew, Goldstein, Taylor, & Siegel, 1994; Twachtman-Cullen, 2000b, 2000c). Critical thinking skills include:

- Getting the main idea
- Interpreting
- Sequencing
- Determining relevance
- Making inferences
- Making predictions and extending information
- Drawing conclusions
- Problem solving
- Reasoning
- Analyzing and synthesizing information
- Evaluating

• Executive function and critical thinking are crucial to higher-level thinking and independent functioning.

Note: Although EF deficits are more readily apparent in more able students with ASD, they are also present in less able students. *IEP teams are urged to give specific attention to EF functioning for all students with ASD, as deficits in this area can easily be mistaken for non-compliance or laziness.*

• Research demonstrates that individuals with ASD present with deficits in *theory of mind* (Baron-Cohen, Tager-Flusberg, & Cohen, 1993; Hobson, 1989; Tager-Flusberg & Sullivan, 1994). Deficits in this domain create problems in using external behavior to understand and predict mental states in others. This difficulty not only creates problems in perspective taking and empathy, but also negatively impacts the student's ability to make sense of another person's behavior.

Present Levels of Performance for Cognitive and Social-Cognitive Skills Should Include:

- A statement indicating the student's strengths in cognitive and/or social-cognitive skills, particularly as they relate to overall functioning in these domains (i.e., executive function, critical thinking, and/or theory of mind).

- A statement regarding the student's weaknesses in specific areas of cognitive and/or social-cognitive skills, particularly as they relate to priority educational needs for the coming year.

- A statement of how the student's disability in cognitive and/or social-cognitive skills impacts his/her involvement and progress in the general curriculum (or for preschool children, in appropriate activities).

- The source(s) of the statement(s) in the PLP.

- Any additional information that can enable the PLP to fulfill its two important functions: 1) *To serve as the basis for generating need-based individualized IEP objectives;* and, 2) *To serve as the standard by which to judge performance/ progress.*

CONTENT AREA:
Executive Function — Using Schedule Systems/ Transitioning

Sample PLP for a 12-year-old student with moderate autism: *According to clinical observation and teacher report, when student is already involved in an activity he is able to function adequately within it. The amount of time it takes him to "settle in," however, is often a problem, as Student has difficulty transitioning from one activity to another, especially when the upcoming activity is unexpected or undesired. He also becomes upset when unanticipated events disrupt his routine. These difficulties affect his ability to participate in important curricular and extra-curricular activities in both his special education resource room and mainstream settings.*

Goal/Objective Templates Based Upon PLP:

Annual Goal: Student will demonstrate improvement in the executive function skill of transitioning from one activity to another as specified in, and measured by short-term objective(s).

Short-term Objective: Given a daily visual schedule, and a direct verbal cue to check it for each of the activities depicted, Student will demonstrate the ability to transition from activity to activity by:

1. Obtaining the appropriate picture card;

2. Moving to the appropriate place; and,

3. Returning the picture card to the "*finished*" box/envelope at the conclusion of the activity,

(Specify criteria) given (prompt levels/fade back plan and generalization protocol). (Specify evaluation procedure and schedule.)

Explanatory notes:

- This objective lends itself to the objective writing format discussed in Chapter 5, whereby different prompt levels are assigned at different points in the year.

- Another way of fostering independence is to move from the *direct* verbal cue specified in the first line of the objective (e.g., *"Check your schedule"*), to an *indirect* verbal cue (e.g., *"What is it time to do?"*).

Recommended Educational Programming Formats:
A, O, P, Q

CONTENT AREA: Executive Function — Planning/Time Management

Sample PLP for a 10-year-old student with AS: *According to informal observation and teacher report, Student is able to perform simple one-step activities adequately. Notwithstanding, she presents with several organizational problems as a result of her EF deficits. For example, when presented with a multi-step activity and no supports, she tends to "bog down" on a particular step, rather than move forward to completion. This difficulty impacts her ability to independently complete assignments in a timely manner, if at all, in her inclusive 4th grade classroom.*

Goal/Objective Templates Based Upon PLP:

Annual Goal: Student will demonstrate improvement in specific areas of executive function as specified in, and measured by short-term objectives.

Short-term Objective 1: Given a visual template depicting the steps in a multi-step activity, Student will complete a (specify number e.g., 3-step, 5-step, etc.) activity, (specify criteria) given (specify prompt levels/fade back plan and generalization protocol). (Specify evaluation procedure/schedule.)

Short-term Objective 2: Given a visual representation of time (e.g., an egg timer), and a visual template depicting the steps in a multi-step activity, Student will complete each component of the activity in a given amount of time, (specify criteria), given (specify prompt levels/fade back plan and generalization protocol). (Specify evaluation procedure and schedule.)

Explanatory note: Prompts may include *direct* verbal cues to look at the clock, or *indirect* cues (e.g., "*How much time do you have left?*").

Recommended Educational Programming Formats: A, C, H, I, J, O, Q

Sample PLP for a 9-year-old student with AS: *According to clinical observation and teacher report, Student is able to manage short-term assignments with an adequate degree of independence; however, when presented with a long-term project involving a number of steps, he has difficulty knowing where to begin. He cannot organize the activity in a logical and sequential manner in order to bring it to completion. In addition, he will often spend too much time on a small aspect of the project, and simply run out of time for the rest of it. These difficulties impact his ability to complete required long-term assignments in a timely manner in his 4th grade inclusive classroom.*

Goal/Objective Templates Based Upon PLP:

Annual Goal: Student will demonstrate improvement in the executive function skills of planning and time management as specified in, and measured by short-term objective(s).

Short-term Objective: Given direct instruction in how to break down long-term assignments, an "end goal" (e.g., project/report), and a step-by-step time line for completion, Student will chain through each component/step in the time allotted, (specify criteria) given (specify prompt levels/fade back plan and generalization protocol). (Specify evaluation procedure and schedule.)

Explanatory notes:

• In order to have a sufficient number of opportunities to work on this objective, we recommend fabricating additional "long-term" projects (e.g., social studies/ science assignments to be completed over a multi-day or week-long period).

• This objective could also be applied to planning future events, such as an in-class holiday party or other activity.

Recommended Educational Programming Formats: B, H, I, O, Q

CONTENT AREA:
Executive Function—Basic Planning

Sample PLP for a 10-year-old student with autism and mental retardation: *Student functions quite well in her special education setting as long as she is told and shown exactly what to do. Her teacher reports, however, that she sometimes appears "at a loss" when directions are given. Her speech-language pathologist notes specific difficulty with time and ordinal concepts (e.g., before/after; first/last). This impacts student's ability to follow directions in both her special education setting, and in the mainstream environments to which she is assigned.*

Goal/Objective Templates Based Upon PLP:

Annual Goal: Student will demonstrate improvement in the executive function skill of planning as specified in, and measured by short-term objectives.

Short-term Objective 1: Given direct instruction and contextually relevant material, Student will demonstrate the ability to understand the language of planning (e.g., *before, after, first, next, last*) by responding appropriately to directives involving these concepts, (specify criteria) given (specify prompt levels/fade back plan and generalization protocol). (Specify evaluation procedure and schedule.)

Short-term Objective 2: Given a calendar and a color-coded overlay representing *past, present,* and *future,* Student will demonstrate the ability to understand these concepts by answering questions involving them, (specify criteria) given (specify prompt levels/fade back plan and generalization protocol). (Specify evaluation procedure and schedule.)

Recommended Educational Programming Formats: A, B, H, I, J, K, L, M, Q

CONTENT AREA:
Executive Function—Self Monitoring

Sample PLP for a 16-year-old student with HFA:
*Student's teachers and parents report that as long as they use
verbal prompts he is able to meet expectations with respect to
completing assignments and keeping track of his belongings.
They also report, however, that he has considerable difficulty
with organizational skills. He frequently fails to bring home the
necessary materials to complete homework assignments, and
often forgets to bring his homework to school when he does complete it. These difficulties impact his ability to effectively meet
requirements across his 11th grade inclusive classroom settings.*

Goal/Objective Templates Based Upon PLP:

Annual Goal: Student will demonstrate improvement in the
use of organizational supports as specified in, and measured
by short-term objective(s).

Short-term Objective: Given direct instruction in the use
of color-coded organizational supports, and a checklist,
Student will monitor materials and assignments across all
academic subjects, (specify criteria) given (specify prompt
levels/fade back plan and generalization protocol). (Specify
evaluation procedure and schedule.)

Explanatory notes:
- Criteria should include not only percentage of opportunities (e.g., 80%), but should also reflect consistency of
  performance (e.g., across 3–5 consecutive days).
- This objective lends itself nicely to the following prompt
  hierarchy: progression over time from direct to indirect
  verbal cues, to nonverbal cues, to expectant time delay, to
  spontaneous use of supports.

- While the type of organizational supports may change in appearance over time (e.g., a written schedule vs. a visual schedule), *by no means do we intend the fading back of prompts to include the fading back of organizational supports.* In fact, we consider these supports to be the "prosthetic devices" that enable organized behavior in students with ASD.

Recommended Educational Programming Formats: A, H, I, J, K, L, M, O, Q

CONTENT AREA:
Executive Function—Impulse Control

Sample PLP for a 5-year-old student with AS: *Despite Student's strengths in vocabulary development, spelling, and reading decoding, his teacher reports that he is "extremely impulsive," citing as an example his constantly blurting out questions and comments during morning circle. His parents note that impulsivity is often a problem at home, as well. According to the teacher, Student's difficulty controlling his impulses is beginning to take its toll with respect to his classmates, as evidenced by their reactions to his disruptions in morning circle. This problem negatively impacts Student's ability to participate appropriately in many of the activities in his inclusive kindergarten classroom, and interferes with his ability to establish relationships with peers.*

Goal/Objective Templates Based Upon PLP:

Annual Goal: Student will demonstrate improvement in impulse control as specified in, and measured by short-term objective(s).

Short-term Objective: Given direct instruction in the use of a visual cue (e.g., red "light" means time to be quiet; green "light" means it's okay to talk), Student will demonstrate improvement in impulse control by reducing the number of interruptions during (specify activity e.g., morning circle) by, (specify criteria e.g., 50% over baseline) given (specify prompt levels/fade back plan and generalization protocol). (Specify evaluation procedure and schedule.)

Explanatory note: It should be obvious that this objective, as written, presumes a prior baseline measure against which progress will be evaluated.

Recommended Educational Programming Formats: A, C, F, L, N, O, Q

CONTENT AREA:
Critical Thinking—Prediction

Sample PLP for a 6-year-old student with PDD-NOS:
Student is able to answer questions about factual material and the here and now. She is also hyperlexic (i.e., evidences advance-level decoding skills in the presence of comprehension difficulty). According to informal assessment and teacher observation, however, Student has difficulty in the area of prediction. Specifically, when presented with the first two steps of a 3-step sequence, she is unable to predict what comes next. Formal assessment has also revealed that Student has difficulty with comprehension of time sequences. These difficulties impact her ability to function in her inclusive classroom setting, as her teacher reports that she frequently becomes overwhelmed when she is unable to extend information and make predictions about events in stories.

Goal/ Objective Templates Based Upon PLP:

Annual Goal: Student will demonstrate improvement in the critical thinking skill of prediction as specified in, and measured by short-term objectives.

Short-term Objective 1: Given direct instruction in sequencing activities, and 3 picture cards in a 4-card sequence, Student will choose the appropriate 4th card from a group of (specify number) choices, (specify criteria) given (specify prompt levels/fade back plan and generalization protocol). (Specify evaluation procedure and schedule.)

Short-term Objective 2: Given direct instruction in sequencing activities, and 3 picture cards in a 4-card sequence, Student will verbally predict what will happen next, (specify criteria) given (specify prompt levels/fade back plan and generalization protocol). (Specify evaluation procedure and schedule.)

214

Short-term Objective 3: Given direct instruction in a story sequence, Student will predict (i.e., answer the question, "*What do you think will happen next?*") across (specify number) stories, (specify criteria) given (specify prompt levels/ fade back plan and generalization protocol). (Specify evaluation procedure and schedule.)

Short-term Objective 4: Given a picture schedule, Student will predict (i.e., answer the question, "*What are we going to do next?*") across all classroom activities, (specify criteria) given (specify prompt levels/fade back plan and generalization protocol). (Specify evaluation procedure and schedule).

Recommended Educational Programming Formats:
A, E, F, G, H, K, L, M, O, Q

CONTENT AREA:
Critical Thinking—Making Inferences

Sample PLP for a 14-year-old student with HFA: *According to formal assessment and teacher report, Student is able to deal effectively with factual material, often scoring well above many of his peers on both standardized and teacher made tests. His ability to make even simple inferences, however, lags far behind. This makes it difficult for Student to deal with essay tests that require him to move beyond a factual level. Moreover, because of his problems with inferential material, he tends to take everything literally. These difficulties have provoked some of his classmates to make fun of him, and have created significant problems for him in academic subjects that require inferential understanding.*

Goal/ Objective Templates Based Upon PLP:

Annual Goal: Student will demonstrate improvement in the critical thinking skill of making inferences as specified in, and measured by short-term objectives.

Short-term Objective 1: Given direct teaching in how to make inferences, and a series of picture cards depicting a variety of common social situations, Student will infer the activity/event depicted, (specify criteria) given (specify prompt levels/fade back plan and generalization protocol). (Specify evaluation procedure and schedule.)

Short-term Objective 2: Given direct teaching and a series of picture cards depicting a variety of common social situations, Student will demonstrate the ability to make inferences by answering inferential questions, (specify criteria) given (specify prompt levels/fade back plan and generalization protocol). (Specify evaluation procedure and schedule.)

Recommended Educational Programming Formats: A, F, G, H, K, L, M, O, Q

216

CONTENT AREA:
Critical Thinking—Problem Solving

Sample PLP for a 6-year-old student with PDD: *Clinical observation indicates that Student participates effectively in activities and events that are predictable and structured. She has a great deal of difficulty, however, coping with activities that do not have a clear beginning and ending. In addition, she becomes highly anxious when there are changes in routine, or when she has to transition from one activity to another. These problems cause her to become overwhelmed, and adversely affect her ability to participate in many of the activities within her preschool classroom.*

Goal/Objective Templates Based Upon PLP:

Annual Goal: Student will demonstrate improved coping skills by applying problem solving strategies as specified in, and measured by short-term objective(s).

Short-term Objective: Given direct instruction in specific problem-solving strategies (specify strategies e.g., asking for a break, asking for "sensory diet" material, etc.) and manual sign cues for using them, Student will apply problem-solving strategies in actual situations, (specify criteria) given (specify prompt levels/fade back plan and generalization protocol). (Specify evaluation procedure and schedule.)

Explanatory notes:

- This objective *requires* the adult to observe the student closely for signs of anxiety, and to present the manual sign cue *before* the student becomes overwhelmed.

- This objective is also appropriate for use with older students, as it lends itself nicely to role-play activities in which students can practice using problem solving strategies outside the "heat of the moment."

Recommended Educational Programming Formats: A, B, C, J, K, L, M, O, Q

Sample PLP for a 16-year-old student with moderate autism: *When given visual supports, and when activities proceed as expected, Student is able to complete assignments in his classroom and work settings in a timely manner. His teacher and vocational supervisor report, however, that he becomes confused and unable to complete his work when even minor problems interrupt his activities. Formal testing via the Test of Problem Solving—Revised (TOPS—R) also indicates difficulty in this area. These problems negatively impact his ability to function independently in both classroom and work-related settings.*

Goal/Objective Templates Based Upon PLP:

Annual Goal: Student will demonstrate improvement in problem solving skills as specified in, and measured by short-term objectives.

Short-term Objective 1: Given direct instruction in the use of a problem solving template, and a series of (specify number) problem scenarios, Student will choose an appropriate solution from (specify number) options presented, (specify criteria) given (specify prompt levels/fade back plan and generalization protocol). (Specify evaluation procedure and schedule.)

Short-term Objective 2: Given direct instruction in the use of a problem solving template, and a series of (specify number) problem scenarios, Student will apply the problem solving strategy appropriate to the situation in structured role-plays with at least 1 peer, (specify criteria) given (specify

prompt levels/fade back plan and generalization protocol).
(Specify evaluation procedure and schedule.)

Recommended Educational Programming Formats:
A, B, K, L, M, N, O, P, Q

Content Area:
Theory of Mind/Perspective Taking

Sample PLP for a 10-year-old student with AS: *According to her teacher, Student manifests strengths in vocabulary, spelling, and reading decoding. Her speech-language pathologist reports that Student has a great deal of difficulty in the area of social cognition. While she does well in situations that do not require her to take the perspective of others, her teacher and parents report that she becomes highly agitated when others don't agree with her. As a result, she is often argumentative both at home and in school. Her accuracy rate on the Test of Problem Solving—Revised (TOPS—R) is 40% for questions that involve perspective taking. Because of these difficulties, Student has problems making friends, and interacting with her teacher and peers in an appropriate manner.*

Goal/Objective Templates Based Upon PLP:

Annual Goal: Student will demonstrate improvement in the elements of perspective taking as specified in, and measured by short-term objectives.

Short-term Objective 1: Given direct instruction in making predictions about mental states (e.g., angry, sad, anxious, etc.), and role-play vignettes involving exaggerated emotional cues, Student will select the card from a group of (specify number) cards presented, that best represents the mental state depicted in the role play scenario, (specify criteria) given (specify prompt levels/fade back plan and generalization protocol). (Specify evaluation procedure and schedule.)

Explanatory note: Moving from the exaggerated cues specified in the objective to more normalized ones is also an excellent way of fading back prompts.

Short-term Objective 2: Given prior direct instruction, demonstration/modeling, and (specify number) cards

depicting mental states (e.g., angry, sad, anxious, etc.),
Student will act out the emotion depicted in structured role-
play vignettes with at least (specify number) peer(s), (specify
criteria) given (specify prompt levels/fade back plan and generalization protocol). (Specify evaluation procedure and
schedule.)

Recommended Educational Programming Formats:
A, C, F, G, K, L, M, N, O, Q

Sample PLP for a 7-year-old student with HFA:
*According to formal assessment, clinical observation, and
teacher report, Student is able to recognize some of the more
apparent emotions in pictures (e.g., happy, sad, angry). He
does not acknowledge these emotions, however, when others
display them, nor does he recognize them when he experiences
them himself. These deficits compromise overall sense making,
and make it difficult for him to make inferences and
predictions about another person's behavior.*

Goal/Objective Templates Based Upon PLP:

Annual Goal: Student will demonstrate improvement in the
ability to connect emotions to events in self and others as
specified in, and measured by short-term objective(s).

Short-term Objective: Given prior direct teaching, manual
sign cues, and a carrier phrase (e.g., "*I feel happy because ...*"
"*He/she feels sad because ...*"), Student will state the appropriate event (i.e., reason) to connect the emotion with the
experience, (specify criteria) given (specify prompt levels/
fade back plan and generalization protocol). (Specify evaluation procedure and schedule.)

Recommended Educational Programming Formats:
A, B, C, E, F, G, K, L, M, O, Q

Miscellaneous Short-term Objective Templates for Cognitive and Social-Cognitive Skills

Short-term Objective 1: Given direct instruction and examples, Student will predict the ending of (specify number) short stories by selecting the appropriate card from a group of (specify number) options, (specify criteria) given (specify prompt levels/fade back plan and generalization protocol). (Specify evaluation procedure and schedule.)

Short-term Objective 2: Given direct instruction in what is meant by the term *relevance*, and (specify number) story scenarios in which information is missing, Student will select the piece of information that is relevant to the story from a group of (specify number) options, (specify criteria) given (specify prompt levels/fade back plan and generalization protocol). (Specify evaluation procedure and schedule.)

Short-term Objective 3: Given direct instruction and examples, and (specify number) short stories, Student will select the appropriate conclusion for each of the stories from a group of (specify number) options, (specify criteria) given (specify prompt levels/fade back plan and generalization protocol). (Specify evaluation procedure and schedule.)

Short-term Objective 4: Given direct instruction and examples, and (specify number) short stories, Student will verbally supply an appropriate conclusion for each of the stories, (specify criteria) given (specify prompt levels/fade back plan and generalization protocol). (Specify evaluation procedure and schedule.)

Short-term Objective 5: Given direct instruction in what is meant by perspective taking, and (specify number) story scenarios in which 2 characters feel *differently* about the *same* situation (i.e., happy vs. sad), Student will demonstrate understanding of their different perspectives by selecting reasons appropriate to the emotional states depicted, and matching them to each character, (specify criteria) given (specify prompt levels/fade back plan and generalization protocol). (Specify evaluation procedure and schedule.)

Explanatory note: Teaching tip number 9 in the list that follows provides detailed information on how to teach the perspective-taking skills presented in Objective 5.

General Teaching Tips & Strategies For Cognitive And Social-Cognitive Skills

1. Visual supports should be considered *executive function props*. We recommend their frequent use in all settings. The following list contains examples of some of the many ways these supports may be used in both the school and home environments:

   - To illustrate activity sequences and multi-step tasks
   - To represent events
   - To demarcate time
   - To delineate tasks and assignments
   - To concretize abstract concepts and choices
   - To cue desirable behavior and language
   - To stabilize information
   - To facilitate self-monitoring
   - To increase understanding
   - To aid working memory

2. Utilize color-coded materials as organizational tools (e.g., files, cue cards, *Post it Notes*, activity boxes, etc.).

3. Provide students with frequent, repetitive language input, along with visual cues, *as events and activities are occurring*, in order to help them make the appropriate connections.

4. Use cause and effect toys to illustrate causal relationships that the child can directly control through his/her own actions.

5. Use sequence cards and children's literature to promote the development of critical thinking skills. For example, to work on prediction using the book, *If You Give A Mouse A Cookie*, ask the question posed in the title, *"If you give a mouse a cookie, what will he ask for next?"*

Continue to ask the question for each item requested, for a veritable powerhouse of prediction opportunities! This activity can even be used with nonverbal children by having them select from a group of objects representing the events in the story, the item that "predicts" what will happen next. Additional books in this series are listed in the *Teaching Resources* section.

6. Frequently point out the emotions of others in naturally occurring situations to help students connect emotional states to activities and events.

7. "Code" the thoughts of the student with ASD in situations involving high emotion (both positive and negative), so that he/she can begin to make connections between his or her own behavior and emotions.

8. Make the connections for the student in situations requiring inferential reasoning that he/she might not be able to make independently. For example, in the book, *Goldilocks and the Three Bears*, neurotypical children readily infer that if Goldilocks is eating from the little bowl, then it must belong to Baby Bear. To ensure that children with ASD make the appropriate connection, we recommend supplying it for them (e.g., *"That must be Baby Bear's bowl, because it's so little."*)

9. Create a perspective-taking game in which two characters (e.g., Sammy and Suzie) react *differently* to the *same* situation. Draw faces on a chalk or laminate board, where one character has a smile, while the other one has a frown. Write the reasons for their disparate reactions on index cards that the student has to match to the emotional state depicted (e.g., happy vs. sad). Consider the following scenario: Situation: *"It's raining. Suzie is frowning, but Sammy is smiling."* Direct the student to find out the reasons why Suzie and Sammy feel differently about the same situation (i.e., the rain) by having

him/her pick a card and match it to the character portraying the appropriate mental state. Sample reasons could include the following:

- *Someone was supposed to go on a picnic. Because of the rain, the picnic has been cancelled.*

- *Someone was supposed to mow the lawn, but won't be able to because it's raining.*

Give the student many opportunities to engage in perspective-taking activities by fabricating several additional scenarios.

10. Use the *Time Timer*, and other visual means of demarcating time (e.g., egg timers) for self-monitoring and time management, as they *visually* depict the passage of time, thus enabling the student to see when he/she has "a lot of" or "a little" time left to complete a task or enjoy a break. (See *Appendix B* for ordering information regarding the *Time Timer*.)

Useful Teaching Resources

(See *Appendix B* for additional information.)

1. *Activities for Mastering Inferences.* By J. G. DeGaetano.

2. *Asperger Syndrome: A Practical Guide for Teachers.* By V. Cumine, J. Leach, & G. Stevenson.

3. *Developing Logical Reasoning.* By J. G. DeGaetano.

4. *Explaining.* By M. M. Toomey.

5. *Helping The Child Who Doesn't Fit In.* By S. Nowicki, Jr. & M. P. Duke.

6. *How To Be A Para Pro: A Comprehensive Training Manual For Paraprofessionals.* By D. Twachtman-Cullen.

7. *If You Give A Moose A Muffin.* By L. J. Numeroff.

8. *If You Give A Mouse A Cookie.* By L. J. Numeroff.

9. *If You Give A Pig A Pancake.* By L. J. Numeroff.

10. *Interactive Language Skills.* By J. G. DeGaetano.

11. *Introducing Inference.* By M. M. Toomey.

12. *Preschool First Sequence Pictures* (sets 1 & 2). By Circuit Publications.

13. *Preschool First Stories.* By M. M. Toomey.

14. *Problem Solving Activities.* By J. G. DeGaetano.

15. *The Problem-Solving Workbook.* By T. Zimmerman.

16. *Talk About Planning.* By M. M. Toomey.

17. *Teaching Children with Autism to Mind-Read: A Practical Guide.* By P. Howlin, S. Baron-Cohen, & J. Hadwin.

18. *Teaching Your Child the Language of Social Success.* By M. Duke, S. Nowicki & E. Martin.

19. *Telling a Story.* By M. M. Toomey.

20. The *Time Timer.* Developed by J. Rogers.

21. *Understanding the Nature of Autism: A Practical Guide.* By J. Janzen.

22. *Visual Strategies for Improving Communication.* By L. Hodgdon.

Epilogue

"None of the Emperor's clothes had been so successful before.

"But he has got nothing on," said a little child.

"Oh listen to the innocent," said its father. And one person whispered to the other what the child had said. "He has nothing on—a child says he has nothing on!"

"But he has nothing on!" at last cried all the people.

Hans Christian Andersen
The Emperor's New Clothes

It is a well-kept, and equally well-known "secret" that a shocking number of IEPs for students with disabilities fall far short of meeting their needs, let alone the letter or spirit of the law that championed their right to a *free appropriate public education*. Indeed, for too long now the education community has averted its eyes so as not to publicly acknowledge that the state of the IEP is consummately similar to that of the mythical Emperor in the Hans Christian Andersen fable!

When we began *our* "journey of a thousand miles" well over two hundred pages ago, we had a threefold purpose in mind. First, we wanted to illustrate the scope of the problem plaguing many present-day IEPs. Toward this end, we offered as evidence of the problem, many examples of poor practice across each of the essential elements of the IEP. Sadly, the one feature common to all of these examples is that each of them portrayed *actual* students, with *actual* disabilities, who required—*but failed to obtain*—educational plans appropriate to their *actual* needs!

Our second purpose—*and the one that we consider central to this book*—was to point the way toward a solution to this pressing problem, since to our way of thinking, a problem acknowledged and defined is one that is well on its way to being solved. In keeping with this purpose, we not only included detailed information and examples for each of the elements of the IEP in need of "resuscitation," but also applied this information to the writing of goal and objective templates for areas of functioning typically neglected in IEPs for students with ASD.

Our final purpose in writing this book was to underscore the critical point that *effective service delivery* is intimately connected to the IEP process. In fact, *appropriate* education can only flow from IEPs that are thoughtfully constructed, and skillfully rendered, because only then will *effective* services be possible.

It is our fondest hope that we have served all three purposes well, and, if so, that we have succeeded in placing into the hands of parents and professionals alike, a resource that will help them repair poorly designed IEPs as a first step in their journey to *effective* service delivery and *appropriate* educational programming for students with autism and related disorders.

Diane Twachtman-Cullen, Ph.D., CCC-SLP

Appendix A

RECOMMENDED EDUCATIONAL PROGRAMMING FORMATS

The following instructional contexts are recommended for both initial skill development and for work related to the generalization of skills:

A. Within the structure of day-to-day school and classroom activities/routines (e.g., for younger students: morning circle, centers, snack, etc.; for older students: morning meeting, leisure activities, work stations, etc.)

B. Within community-based activities (e.g., field trips, community-based instruction, etc.)

C. Within structured social, play, and/or leisure activities and routines

D. Within songs, nursery rhymes, chants, and like activities

E. Within felt/magnet board activities

F. Within interactive story routines involving books (e.g., reciprocal reading), play figures, and/or pictures

G. Within narrative activities

H. Within structured academic tasks

I. Within long-term projects/assignments

J. Within art activities

K. Within 1:1 teaching situations

L. Within small group activities

M. Within therapy sessions

N. Within structured role-plays

O. Within naturally occurring events and activities

P. Within pre-vocational and vocational activities

Q. Within extended environments (e.g., home, extra curricular activities, after school programming, etc.)

Appendix B

Teaching resources are listed alphabetically by title.

Activities for Mastering Inferences. By: J. G. DeGaetano. Published by: Great Ideas for Teaching; Wrightsville Beach, NC. ISBN # 1-88614886143-49-8.

Asperger Syndrome: A Practical Guide for Teachers. By: V. Cumine, J. Leach, & G. Stevenson. Published by: David Fulton Publishers; London. ISBN # 1-85346-499-6.

Can-Do Oral-Motor Fun and Games. By: J.P. DeNinno & K. A. Gill. Published by: Super Duper Publications; Greenville, SC. 1-800-277-8737.

Comic Strip Conversations. By: C. Gray. Published by: Future Horizons; Arlington, TX. 1-800-489-0727.

Concept Acquisition Procedures for Preschoolers (CAPP): Levels 1, 2, & 3. By: C. Weiner. Published by: ECL Publications. (623) 974-4560.

Conceptbuilding: Developing Meaning Through Narratives and Discussion. By: P. Reichardt. Published by: Thinking Publications; Eau Claire, WI. 1-800-225-GROW. <u>www.ThinkingPublications.com</u> ISBN # 0-930599-71-3.

Developing Logical Reasoning. By: J. G. DeGaetano. Published by: Great Ideas for Teaching, Inc., Wrightsville Beach, NC. ISBN # 1-886143-45-5.

Dyspraxia: A Guide for Teachers and Parents. By: K. Ripley, B. Daines, & J. Barrett. Published by: David Fulton Publishers; London. ISBN # 1-85346-444-9.

Early Communication Skills. By: C. Lynch & J. Kidd. Published by: Winslow Press Ltd. <u>www.winslow-press-co.uk</u> ISBN # 0-86388-223-4.

Excell: Experiences in Context for Early Language Learning. By: C. B. Raack. Published by: Communication Skill Builders; Tuscon, AZ. ISBN # 0-88450-372-0.

Expanding and Combining Sentences. By: M. M. Toomey. Published by: Circuit Publications; P.O. Box 1201; Marblehead, MA. ISBN # 0-923573-28-3.

Explaining. By: M. M. Toomey. Published by: Circuit Publications; P.O. Box 1201; Marblehead, MA. ISBN # 0-923573-20-8.

Figurative Language: A Comprehensive Program. By: K. A. Gorman-Gard. Published by Thinking Publications; Eau Claire, WI. 1-800-225-GROW. www.ThinkingPublications.com ISBN # 0-930599-72-1.

Great Therapy Ideas! Oral Sensory-Motor Tool-Toys Techniques. By: C. Boshart, H. Demetrion, C. Haislip, T. Harrison, J. Jared, L. Kelly, M. Schueller, & T. Szypulski. Published by: Speech Dynamics; Temecula, CA. 1-800-337-9049.

Helping the Child Who Doesn't Fit In. By: S. Nowicki Jr. & M. P. Duke. Published by: Peachtree Publishers, Ltd.; Atlanta, GA. ISBN # 1-56145-025-1.

How To Be A Para Pro: A Comprehensive Training Manual For Paraprofessionals. By: D. Twachtman-Cullen. Published by: Starfish Specialty Press. 1-877-STARFISH. www.starfishpress.com ISBN # 0-9666529-1-6.

If You Give a Moose a Muffin. By: L. J. Numeroff. Published by: A Laura Geringer book, an imprint of Harper Collins Publishers. ISBN # 0-06-024405-4.

If You Give a Mouse a Cookie. By: L. J. Numeroff. Published by: Harper Collins Publishers. ISBN # 0-06-024586-7.

If You Give a Pig a Pancake. By: L. J. Numeroff. Published by: A Laura Geringer book, an imprint of Harper Collins Publishers. ISBN # 0-06-026686-4.

Interactive Language Skills. By: J. G. DeGaetano. Published by: Great Ideas for Teaching. ISBN # 1-886143-32-3.

Introducing Inference. By: M. M. Toomey. Published by: Circuit Publications; P.O. Box 1201; Marblehead, MA.

Listen My Children and You Shall Hear. By: B. Kratvoville. Published by: Pro-ed. 1-800-897-3202.

Listening, Understanding, Remembering, Verbalizing! By: J. G. DeGaetano. Published by: Great Ideas for Teaching; Wrightsville Beach, NC. ISBN # 1-886143-46-3.

More Social Skills Stories: Very Personal Picture Stories for Readers and Nonreaders K-12. By: A. M. Johnson. Published by: Mayer-Johnson Company; Solana Beach, CA. ISBN # 1-884135-30-7.

Mouth Madness: Oral-Motor Activities for Children. By: C. Orr. Published by: Therapy Skill Builders; San Antonio, TX. 1-800-228-0752. ISBN # 012785028-7.

Narrative Toolbox: Blueprints for Storybuilding. By: P. Hudson-Nechkash. Published by: Thinking Publications; Eau Claire, WI.

1-800-225-4769. www.ThinkingPublications.com
ISBN # 1-888222-61-1.

New Social Stories Illustrated. By: C. Gray. Published by: Future Horizons; Arlington, TX. 1-800-489-0727. ISBN # 1885477-66-x.

Oral-Motor Activities for Young Children. By: E. Mackie. Published by: Linguisystems; East Moline, IL. 1-800-776-4332. ISBN # 0-7606-0107-0.

Oral-Motor Techniques in Articulation and Phonological Therapy. By: P. Marshalla. Published by: Marshalla Speech and Language; Kirkland, WA. www.pammarshalla.com ISBN # 0-9707060-3-0.

Play and Imagination in Children with Autism. By: P. J. Wolfberg. Published by: Teachers College Press. New York, NY. ISBN # 0-8077-3814-x.

Preschool First Sequence Pictures (Sets 1 & 2). Published by: Circuit Publications; P.O. Box 1201; Marblehead, MA. ISBN # 0-923573-35-6.

Preschool First Stories. By: M. M. Toomey. Published by: Circuit Publications; P.O. Box 1201; Marblehead, MA. ISBN # 0-923573-43-7.

Problem Solving Activities. By: J. G. DeGaetano. Published by: Great Ideas for Teaching; Wrightsville Beach, NC. ISBN # 1-8861143-35-8.

Problem-Solving Workbook, The. By: T. Zimmerman. Published by: The Center for Applied Psychology, Inc.; King of Prussia, PA. 1-800-962-1141. ISBN # 1-882732-31-6.

Social Skills Activities for Special Children. By: D. Mannix. Published by: The Center for Applied Research in Education; W. Nyack, NY. ISBN # 0-87628-868-9.

Social Skills Stories: Functional Picture Stories for Readers and Nonreaders K-12. By: A. M. Johnson & J. L. Susnik. Published by: Mayer-Johnson Company; Solana Beach, CA. (619) 550-0084. ISBN # 1-884135-21-8.

Social Skill Strategies: A Social-Emotional Curriculum for Adolescents (Book A). By: N. Gajewski, P. Hirn, & P. Mayo. Published by: Thinking Publications; Eau Claire, WI. 1-800-225-GROW. ISBN # 1-888222-27-1.

Talk About Planning. By: M. M. Toomey. Published by: Circuit Publications; P.O. Box 1201; Marblehead, MA. ISBN # 0-923573-39-9.

Teaching Children with Autism to Mind-Read: A Practical Guide. By: P. Howlin, S. Baron-Cohen, & J. Hadwin. Published by: John Wiley & Sons. ISBN # 0-471-97623-7.

Teaching Spontaneous Communication to Autistic and Developmentally Handicapped Children. By: L. R. Watson, C. Lord, B. Schaffer, & E. Schopler. Published by: Irvington; New York, NY. ISBN # 0-89079-528-2.

Teaching Your Child the Language of Social Success. By: M. Duke, S. Nowicki, & E. Martin. Published by: Peachtree Press; Atlanta, GA. ISBN # 1-56145-126-6.

Telling a Story. By: M. M. Toomey. Published by: Circuit Publications; P.O. Box 1201; Marblehead, MA. ISBN # 0-923573-21-6.

Themestorming. By: J. Becker, K. Reid, P Steinhaus, & P. Wieck. Published by: Gryphon House; Beltsville, MD. ISBN # 0-87659-170-5.

This is the One That I Want. By: L. G. Richman. Published by: Mayer-Johnson Company; Solana Beach, CA. (619) 550-0084. ISBN # 0-9609160-1-6.

The *Time Timer.* Developed by: J. Rogers. Available from: Generaction, Inc. 1-877-771-8463. www.timetimer.com

Understanding the Nature of Autism: A Practical Guide. By: J. Janzen. Published by: Therapy Skill Builders; San Antonio, TX. 1-800-228-0752. ISBN # 0761643796.

Visual Strategies for Improving Communication. By: L. Hodgdon. Published by: Quirk Roberts Publishing (810) 879-2598. ISBN # 0-9616786-1-5.

*Original Social Stories and *New Social Stories* have been discontinued as separate manuals and republished under the title: *New Social Stories Illustrated.*

Note: If some of the above resources are difficult to find, they may be obtained through a variety of sources, including the Library of Speech Pathology book club (717-918-4120).

References

Adams, L. (1998). Oral-motor and motor-speech characteristics of children with autism. *Focus on Autism and Other Developmental Disabilities, 13*(2), 108–112.

Baron-Cohen, S., Tager-Flusberg, H., & Cohen, D. J. (1993). *Understanding other minds: Perspectives from autism.* Oxford, England: Oxford University Press.

Berkell, D. E. (1992). Instructional planning: Goals and practice. In D. E. Berkell (Ed.), *Autism: Identification, education, and treatment* (pp. 89–105). Hillsdale, NJ: Laurence Erlbaum Associates.

Board of Education v. Rowley, 458 U.S. 176 (1982).

Boshart, C. A. (1998). *Oral-motor analysis and remediation techniques.* Temecula, CA: Speech Dynamics.

Carr, E. G., & Kologinsky, E. (1983). Acquisition of sign language by autistic children II: Spontaneity and generalization effects. *Journal of Applied Behavior Analysis, 16,* 297–314.

Cayne, B., et al. (Eds.). (1989). *The new lexicon Webster's dictionary of the English language* (Encyclopedic ed.). New York: Lexicon Publications.

Costello, R. B., et al. (Eds.). (1991). *Random house Webster's college dictionary.* New York: Random House.

Covey, S. R. (1989/1990). *The 7 habits of highly effective people: Powerful lessons in personal change.* New York: Fireside, by Simon & Schuster.

Curcio, F. (1978). Sensorimotor functioning and communication in mute autistic children. *Journal of Autism and Childhood Schizophrenia, 8,* 281–292.

Drew P. v. Clarke County School District, 877 F.2d 927 (11th Cir. 1989).

Florida Department of Education. (2000). *Developing quality individual educational plans: A guide for instructional personnel and families* (Rev. ed.). Tallahassee, FL: Author.

Gena, A., Krantz, P. J., McClannahan, L. D., & Poulson, C. L. (1996). Training and generalization of affective behavior displayed by youth with autism. *Journal of Applied Behavior Analysis, 29*(3), 291–304.

Gaylord-Ross, R. J., Haring, T. J., Breen, C., & Pitts-Conway, V. (1984). The training and generalization of social interaction skills with autistic youth. *Journal of Applied Behavior Analysis, 17*(2), 229–247.

Gillberg, C., & Ehlers, S. (1998). High-Functioning people with autism and Asperger syndrome: A literature review. In E. Schopler, G. B. Mesibov, & L. J. Kunce (Eds.), *Asperger syndrome or high-functioning autism?* (pp. 79–106). New York: Plenum Press.

Goldstein, G., Minshew, N. J., & Siegel, D. J. (1994). Age differences in academic achievement in high-functioning autistic individuals. *Journal of Clinical and Experimental Neuropsychology, 16*(5), 671–680.

Gray, C. (1994/2000). *New social stories illustrated.* Arlington, TX: Future Horizons.

Grice, H. (1975). Logic and conversation. In D. Davidson & G. Harmon (Eds.), *The logic of grammar.* Encino, CA: Dickinson.

Hobson, P. (1989). Beyond cognition: A theory of autism. In G. Dawson (Ed.), *Autism: Nature, diagnosis, and treatment* (pp. 22–48). New York: The Guilford Press.

Ihrig, K., & Wolchik, S. A. (1988). Peer versus adult models and autistic children's learning: Acquisition, generalization, and maintenance. *Journal of Autism and Developmental Disorders, 18*(1), 67–49.

Kaye, K. (1982). *The mental and social life of babies: How parents create persons.* Chicago: University of Chicago Press.

Klin, A., & Volkmar, F. R. (2000). Treatment and intervention guidelines for individuals with Asperger syndrome. In A. Klin, F. R. Volkmar, & S. S. Sparrow (Eds.), *Asperger syndrome* (pp. 340–366). New York: The Guilford Press.

Koegel, R. L., Koegel, L. K., & O'Neill, R. (1989). Generalization in the treatment of autism. In L. V. McReynolds & J. E. Sprandlin (Eds.), *Generalization strategies in the treatment of communication disorders* (pp. 116–131). Toronto: B. C. Decker.

Landa, R. (2000). Social language use in Asperger syndrome and high-functioning autism. In A. Klin, F. R. Volkmar, & S.S. Sparrow (Eds.), *Asperger syndrome* (pp. 125–155). New York: The Guilford Press.

Lentz, K. (2001). *Hopes and dreams: An IEP field guide for parents and children with autism spectrum disorders.* (Available from Kirby Lentz, 1329 4th Avenue North, Onalaska, WI 54650–9141; kblentz@msn.com).

238

Mackie, E. (1996). *Oral–motor activities for young children*. East Moline, IL: Linguisystems.

Mager, R. F. (1997a). *Measuring instructional results (or Got a match): How to find out if your instructional objectives have been achieved* (3rd ed.). Atlanta, GA: The Center for Effective Performance.

Mager, R. F. (1997b). *Preparing instructional objectives: A critical tool in the development of effective instruction* (3rd ed.). Atlanta, GA: The Center for Effective Performance.

Martin, R. (1996). *What schools forget to tell parents about their rights*. Arlington, TX: Future Horizons.

Martin, R. (n.d.). *34 code of federal regulations 300. Appendix A.* Retrieved August 1, 2001, from http://www.reedmartin.com/appendixa.html

Minshew, N. (1996). Autism. In B. O. Berg (Ed.), *Principles of child neurology* (pp. 1713–1729). New York: McGraw-Hill.

Minshew, N. J., Goldstein, G., Taylor, H. G., & Siegel, D. J. (1994). Academic achievement in high functioning autistic individuals. *Journal of Clinical and Experimental Neuropsychology, 16*(2), 261–270.

Mundy, P., & Sigman, M. (1989). The theoretical implications of joint attention deficits in autism. *Development and Psychopathology, 1,* 173–183.

Olley, G. J., & Stevenson, S. E. (1989). Preschool curriculum for children with autism: Addressing early social skills. In. G. Dawson (Ed.), *Autism: Nature, diagnosis, and treatment* (pp. 346–366). New York: The Guilford Press.

Ozonoff, S. (1997). Components of executive function in autism and other disorders. In J. Russell (Ed.), *Autism as an executive disorder* (pp. 179–211). Oxford, NY: Oxford University Press.

Peeters, T., & Gillberg, C. (1999). *Autism: Medical and educational aspects* (2nd ed.). London: Whurr.

Pennington, B. F., Bennetto, L., McAleer, O., & Roberts, R. J., Jr. (1996). Executive function and working memory: Theoretical and measurement issues. In G. R. Lyon & N. A. Krasnegor (Eds.), *Attention, memory, and executive function* (pp. 327–348). Baltimore: Paul H. Brookes.

Powers, M. D. (1992). Early intervention for children with autism. In D. E. Berkell (Ed.), *Autism: Identification, education, and treatment* (pp 225–252). Hillsdale, NJ: Lawrence Erlbaum Associates.

Rincover A., & Koegel, R. L. (1975). Setting generality and stimulus control in autistic children. *Journal of Applied Behavior Analysis, 8,* 235–246.

Rogers, S. J., & Bennetto, L. (2000). Intersubjectivity in autism: The roles of imitation and executive function. In A. M. Wetherby & B. M. Prizant (Eds.), *Autism spectrum disorders: A transactional developmental perspective* (pp. 79–107). Baltimore: Paul H. Brookes.

Sevcik, R. A., & Romski, M. A. (1997). Comprehension and language acquisition: Evidence from youth with cognitive disabilities. In L. B. Adamson & M. A. Romski (Eds.), *Communication and language acquisition: Discoveries from atypical development* (pp. 187–202). Baltimore: Paul H. Brookes.

Siegel, L. M. (2001). *The complete IEP guide: How to advocate for your special ed child* (2nd ed.). Berkeley, CA: Nolo.

Sigman, M., Mundy, P., Sherman, T., & Ungerer, J. (1986). Social interactions of autistic, mentally retarded, and normal children and their caregivers. *Journal of Child Psychology and Psychiatry, 27,* 647–656.

Stokes, T. F., & Osnes, P. G. (1988). The developing applied technology of generalization and maintenance. In R. Horner, G. Dunlap, & R. L. Koegel (Eds.), *Generalization and maintenance* (pp. 5–19). Baltimore: Paul H. Brookes.

Tager-Flusberg, H., & Sullivan, K. (1994). Predicting and explaining behavior: A comparison of autistic, mentally retarded, and normal children. *Journal of Child Psychology and Psychiatry, 35*(6), 1059–1075.

Tantam, D. (2000). Adolescence and adulthood in individuals with Asperger syndrome. In A. Klin, F. R. Volkmar, & S. S. Sparrow (Eds.), *Asperger syndrome* (pp. 367–399). New York: The Guilford Press.

Taylor, B. A., & Harris, S. L. (1995). Teaching children with autism to seek information: Acquisition of novel information and generalization of responding. *Journal of Applied Behavior Analysis, 28*(1), 3–14.

Twachtman-Cullen, D. (1998). Language and communication in high-functioning autism and Asperger syndrome. In E. Schopler, G. B. Mesibov, & L. J. Kunce (Eds.), *Asperger syndrome or high-functioning autism?* (pp. 199–225). New York: Plenum Press.

Twachtman-Cullen, D. (2000a). *How to be a para pro: A comprehensive training manual for paraprofessionals.* Higganum, CT: Starfish Specialty Press.

Twachtman-Cullen, D. (2000b). More able children with autism spectrum disorders: Sociocommunicative challenges and guidelines for enhancing abilities. In A. M. Wetherby & B. M. Prizant (Eds.), *Autism spectrum disorders: A transactional developmental perspective* (pp. 225–249). Baltimore: Paul H. Brookes.

Twachtman-Cullen, D. (2000c). Asperger syndrome: What we don't know we cannot address. *The Journal of Developmental and Learning Disorders, 4*(1), 83–107.

Twachtman-Cullen, D. (2001, February 23). Paraprofessional support: It's a two-way street. *The Special Educator, 16*(14), 1, 10.

Twachtman-Cullen, D. (2001). A formula for designing highly effective IEPs for students with autism spectrum disorders. *Proceedings of the Autism Society of America National Conference* (pp. 115–117). Arlington, TX: Future Horizons.

Wetherby, A. M., & Prutting, C. A. (1984). Profiles of communicative and cognitive-social abilities in autistic children. *Journal of Speech and Hearing Research, 27*(3), 364–377.

Wolfberg, P. (1999). *Play and imagination in children with autism.* New York: Teachers College Press.

Woods, T. S. (1987). The technology of instruction: A behavior analytic approach. In D. J. Cohen & A. M. Donnellan (Eds.), *Handbook of autism and pervasive developmental disorders* (pp. 251–272). New York: Wiley.

Wright, P. W. D. & Wright, P. D. (1999/2000). *Wrightslaw: Special education law.* Hartfield, VA: Harbor House Law Press.

241

Subject Index

Page numbers for tables and forms are listed in italics